LICHTENSTEIN in new york

A POP ART LIFE

Mark P. Bernardo

ROARING FORTIES
P R E S S

Berkeley, California

LICHTENSTEIN
in new YORK

A POP ART LIFE

Roaring Forties Press
1053 Santa Fe Avenue
Berkeley, CA 94706
www.roaringfortiespress.com

Cover and interior design by Nigel Quinney.
Cover photograph © Bernard Gotfryd.
Back cover photograph © iStock / Lisa-Blue.

Library of Congress Cataloging-in-Publication Data
Names: Bernardo, Mark P., 1969- author.
Title: Lichtenstein in New York : a pop art life / Mark P.
Bernardo.
Description: Berkeley, California : Roaring Forties Press, 2017. | In-
cludes bibliographical references and index.
Identifiers: LCCN 2016057636 | ISBN 9781938901553 (paperback)
Subjects: LCSH: Lichtenstein, Roy, 1923-1997. | Artists--United
States--Biography. | Art and society--New York (State)--New York
--History--20th century. | New York (N.Y.)--Biography. | BISAC:
BIOGRAPHY & AUTOBIOGRAPHY / Artists, Architects, Photogra-
phers. | ART / American / General. | ART / Popular Culture.
Classification: LCC N6537.L5 B47 2017 | DDC 709.2 [B] --dc23 LC
record available at https://lccn.loc.gov/2016057636

978-1-938901-55-3 (print)
978-1-938901-69-0 (ebook)

CONTENTS

PREFACE AND ACKNOWLEDGMENTS

When I first pitched this book to Roaring Forties Press, and during the early period of my research, my goal was relatively simple: to examine the career of one of the mid-twentieth-century's most important artists and to discover how that career was influenced by, and in turn exerted its own influence on, New York City.

My fascination with Roy Lichtenstein stemmed both from my background in comic book publishing and from what struck me as a curious dearth of definitive biographical material on the artist. There is a fairly substantial wealth of critical analysis of his work, but little about the man himself. Other midcentury giants such as Andy Warhol and Jackson Pollock have biographies, but not Lichtenstein, even though his career was longer than theirs.

In the course of my research—which involved unearthing contemporary newspaper and magazine accounts of Pop Art's mid-1960s heyday as well as sifting through scholarly tomes on the Pop phenomenon, the 1960s in general, New York City's history, and the Silver Age of comics—the project evolved into something more.

This book in no way purports to be that definitive cradle-to-tomb biography of Roy Lichtenstein that I—and surely many others—would love to see. But what this book does provide, or so I hope, is a more detailed and well-balanced portrait than has been published before, a portrait that not only describes the course of his life but also explores his relationship to his work and probes the controversy that often surrounded that work. This volume also chronicles how America (particularly New York City) and Americans (particularly Lichtenstein) wrought momentous changes in the art world in the second half of the twentieth century. With a career spanning the 1950s' heyday of the Abstract Expressionists to the 1990s' neo-Pop of Keith Haring and Jean-Michel Basquiat, Lichtenstein is the perfect lens through which to look at a revolutionary era in art.

It is inevitable that at some point in reading this, the reader will notice that this is a book about an artist that contains no art by that artist. The reason for this goes back to that curious lack of biographical material on Lichtenstein. As numerous sources contacted for assistance with this book have confirmed, the Roy Lichtenstein Foundation, managed by the late artist's widow, is notoriously and rigidly tight with rights and permissions, not only for reproductions of Lichtenstein's artwork but even for pictures of the artist himself. (Some of Lichtenstein's detractors, such as those champions of the original comic book illustrators whose four-color panels were appropriated for Lichtenstein's canvases, might find this ironic.) For reasons of its own, the foundation seemed not to want to cooperate with my publisher or me on the manuscript. As a result, the book you are about to read is essentially an unauthorized—albeit heavily researched—biography. Of course, unauthorized biographies have their own merits, having no agenda except the author's, which in this case is not only to deliver that previously mentioned well-balanced portrait but to do so in a way that engages and informs both art world novices and Pop Art aficionados.

A Google search will turn up any of the works mentioned in this book, and many New York City museums (and a few other city landmarks, as you'll discover in chapter 8) offer a glimpse of some of the most famous works. Assuredly, inspiring the reader to make such pilgrimages is another goal of this book. For those interested not just in Lichtenstein's art but in seeing it next to the original comics art that it was based on, I highly recommend David Barsalou's remarkable website, Deconstructing Roy Lichtenstein (https://www.flickr.com/photos/deconstructing-roy-lichtenstein/; http://davidbarsalou.homestead.com/LICHTENSTEINPROJECT.html; https://www.facebook.com/groups/230408213304/), which was immensely helpful in providing background detail for this book. I am also indebted to David for providing some of the art in this book.

As the reader will discover, comics art (or art from advertisements) appears at the start of several of the following chapters. The reason for including these wonderful illustrations is *not* to draw direct parallels between Lichtenstein's work and the work of artists working in the comics industry. They are included for three different reasons. One is to provide a visual acknowledgment of the undeniable fact that Lichtenstein (in his best-known canvases) and these other artists were working in a similar vein, producing self-evidently similar images, albeit for different reasons. The second is to evoke through the selection of the images that appear at the start of each chapter something of the tenor, flavor, and preoccupations of American life in the period covered in that chapter. And the third reason is that, like Lichtenstein's own work, the comics art is simply a pleasure to look at—full of life, wit, adventure, innovation, and those other qualities that one dares to hope are enduring facets of all kinds of American art.

This book would not have been possible without the work of numerous art critics and other writers who have covered Roy Lichtenstein and his decades-long career, among them Fairfield Porter, Lisa Phillips, Michael Lobel, Max Kozloff, Paul Richard, Dorothy Seiberling, John Canaday, Grace Glueck, Hilton Kramer, and Calvin Tomkins, as well as many others whose insights helped me form a more complete picture of this enigmatic artist and his work. I owe many thanks to the aforementioned David Barsalou for his invaluable assistance to my research and for his advocacy of the comics illustrators whose own contributions to Lichtenstein's canon might have otherwise been overlooked. Much gratitude is due to Deirdre Greene and Nigel Quinney at Roaring Forties Press, who rolled the dice years ago on a first-time author and steered this project to the finish line through some significant obstacles. Thanks also to my high school and college art and art history instructors, who stoked the fires of interest way back when, and to my parents, who were way more supportive than many would have been when I expressed an interest in pursuing a career making comic books in the big city.

Finally, to my wife Holly, thank you as always for your love, support, and unfailing encouragement.

LICHTENSTEIN in NEW YORK

1

PAINTING THE TOWN POP

ROY LICHTENSTEIN'S LOVE AFFAIR WITH NEW YORK

If New York City is the crossroads of the world, then Times Square is the crossroads of New York City. Every day, more than half a million people pass through the huge Times Square subway station at 42nd Street—commuters on their way from home to office and back, suburbanites out for a night on Broadway, out-of-town visitors from every corner of the country and across the globe emerging for the first time into the bustling heart of America's most dynamic city.

Bringing with them a wide-eyed sense of wonder, the visitors may be more likely than the notoriously jaded locals to take notice of the mural near the main entrance at 42nd Street and Broadway—a tribute to New York and its boundless sense of ambition and ingenuity, rendered in the distinctive style and idiom of one of Gotham's favorite artistic sons.

In 1994, toward the end of his life, Roy Lichtenstein— the native-born New Yorker who in the 1960s became one of the pillars of the Pop Art movement—was commissioned to create the sprawling work by New York's Metropolitan Transit Authority. Standing 6 feet high and spanning 53 feet in length, the mural depicts a futuristic city skyline, with rocket ships as subways. It is based on an architectural exhibit from the 1964 World's Fair in Flushing Meadows, Queens— perhaps not coincidentally, the event where Lichtenstein's work and that of the other Pop artists was first unveiled on an international stage. The figure of sci-fi space hero Buck Rogers, over whose shoulder viewers glimpse the shining city of the future, makes the work distinctively Lichtenstein's—even though, some may argue, the image itself may have originally come from a long-forgotten cartoonist or commercial illustrator.

Lichtenstein is the only one of that vanguard of Pop artists to be born in New York City—his well-known contemporaries Andy Warhol, Robert Rauschenberg, James Rosenquist, and Jim Dine hailed from Pennsylvania, Texas, North Dakota, and Ohio, respectively. And although Lichtenstein rarely made the city a subject of his work, the influence that its culture had on him, particularly in the vital years between the late 1950s and early 1960s, was tremendous. For New York was not only the American capital of modern art; it was the center of advertising and consumerism, and the country's foremost incubator of popular culture. Lichtenstein's most famous canvases, using the imagery of comic strips, advertising art, and all manner of mass-produced printed material, melded fine art with commercial illustration styles in a way that none before him had envisioned. It is a style whose inspiration is firmly rooted in the commercial culture of New York City, and it makes Lichtenstein a truly unique product of that city.

Like many Americans, Lichtenstein's life experiences did lead him, for a time, far from the city of his birth. He attended college at Ohio State University in Columbus; his studies were interrupted by a tour of duty in the US Army, which took him from basic training in Texas and pilot training in Mississippi to overseas combat in Germany during World War II. He married his first wife in Ohio, where he also began his artistic career as a teacher. However, the call of his hometown proved impossible to ignore.

"Roy was always trying to get back to the New York area," his second wife and widow, Dorothy Lichtenstein, told an interviewer in 2004, "and in 1960 he was able to get a job teaching at Rutgers University in New Jersey. And there was a group of interesting and lively people there, including the artists Allan Kaprow and George Segal. Roy had a feeling that if he'd still had a job teaching out in the boondocks, he might have done his first Pop work, but not carried on. He felt there was something that comes from response and encouragement that fuels you to go further than you might in a vacuum."

In his work and in his life, Lichtenstein always returned to Manhattan, almost as if he knew that only the most cosmopolitan city in the world, the most sophisticated art market, would respond to the work he was producing. As a graduate student at Ohio State, he visited New York galleries for inspiration. By the 1950s, as he embarked on his career as a professional artist, he was making regular treks from his home in Ohio to the galleries and museums of Manhattan, earnestly peddling his early work to the movers and shakers of the art world. By the beginning of the 1960s, the rise of daring new American art styles had spawned a new generation of avant-garde gallery owners such as Leo Castelli, Ileana Sonnabend, Ivan Karp, Betty Parsons, and Sidney Janis, who saw in artists like Roy Lichtenstein and his contemporaries something different—styles that were strange yet fascinating, controversial yet exuding mass appeal; styles that were bringing the figure back to art in a way that was not European but distinctly, defiantly American. All these visionaries called New York home during that momentous postwar era when the city was staking its claim as the art world's vibrant new center.

New York City achieved this status largely due to these gallery owners, who took a chance first on the "Action Painting" of Jackson Pollock, Willem de Kooning, and the other originators of Abstract Expressionism, and later on their brash successors—led by Lichtenstein, Warhol, and the others who practiced the discipline that was first dubbed "new realism" and was later known by its more enduring name, "Pop Art."

The early 1960s were the heyday of Pop Art, with Manhattan the undisputed capital, and Lichtenstein's most memorable art sprang from that richly creative era. But although Lichtenstein moved in the social circle of that world, he was never truly of it. While the colorful Warhol forged himself into a distinctly modern type of celebrity, Lichtenstein, a family man with a work ethic instilled in him by his middle-class upbringing on the Upper West Side, seemed more content to let his work speak for him, even though to this day many are still debating what the work was actually saying—and some critics, including those whose own work served as source material for those iconic canvases, continue to openly question whether his work deserves accolades at all.

The subject matter of his seminal works in the early 1960s ran the gamut of comic book genres from war (*Bratatat!*, *Whaam!*, *Jet Pilot*) and romance (*Vicki! I—I Thought I Heard Your Voice!*; *Good Morning . . . Darling!*; *Blonde Waiting*) to superheroes and villains (*Image Duplicator*, *Mad Scientist*). As public interest in Pop Art waned in the latter part of the decade and into the 1970s, Lichtenstein found muses outside the world of comics, from old masters paintings and mirrors to North American Indian art. Throughout his long career, Lichtenstein's creative juices were stoked by the city around him—his *Head* sculptures emerging from the mannequins of the West Side hat manufacturing district he briefly called home, his *Entablature* series a tribute to the baroque ornamentation of Manhattan skyscrapers, and his enameled early sculptures inspired by New York's ubiquitous metal subway signs.

As the twentieth century moved toward the twenty-first, Lichtenstein was no longer a young rebel in a controversial artistic movement but an established icon, frequently working on commissioned pieces for corporate patrons and civic organizations.

Lichtenstein lived to a ripe old age, producing art almost to the end, and his brushstrokes are all over New York City. His work hangs in museums such as the Metropolitan Museum of Art, the Solomon R. Guggenheim Museum, and the Museum of Modern Art, where the Pop Art movement was officially christened in 1962. Much of the commissioned public work of his later years is still evident in the city, including the Times Square subway mural and the elaborate *Mural with Blue Brushstroke* in the lobby of the AXA Equitable Center in midtown Manhattan.

Lichtenstein in New York: A Pop Art Life is not only a biography but also a chronicle of his times and his city, exploring the evolving nature of culture and art and how each influences the other. It also touches on some of the persistent issues that accompany any consideration of Lichtenstein's career: Where is the line between plagiarism and homage? Between "high art" and "low art"? Between someone who "draws" and someone who is an "artist"?

Through the remarkable life and prolific career of the city's only native Pop artist, it becomes clear that New York City in the mid-twentieth century was the only place in the world that could produce such a groundbreaking artistic movement, and the only place that could ever be home for its most recognizable practitioner. Fittingly, as New York gave to Lichtenstein, Lichtenstein gave back to New York. From Battery Park to Times Square, from the corporate towers of midtown to the public plazas of Central Park, and in museums and galleries from SoHo to Southampton, Roy Lichtenstein's artwork stands as a colorful tribute to a simpler time and place, and a living testament to the unbreakable bonds between an artist and his city.

2

SCHOOLBOY, SOLDIER, TEACHER

AN ARTIST COMES OF AGE

The decade known as the Roaring Twenties was in full swing by 1923, the year Roy Lichtenstein was born, when the popular Charleston song-and-dance craze took hold of a society starved for a party atmosphere amid the puritanical era of Prohibition. The recent war was fading from memory in the United States, even while Europe was precariously poised for a long descent into another ruinous conflict. New York City, always slightly ahead of the national curve culturally, overturned its Prohibition laws that year, motivating Washington to send in federal agents to enforce the national ban on alcohol. While New Yorkers were dancing and drinking at the speakeasies, Babe Ruth, whose services had been purchased in 1919 from the Boston Red Sox, was slugging home runs for the Yankees and the Harlem Renaissance was in full flower, with upper Manhattan becoming a mecca for the legends of jazz.

New York, however, had yet to emerge as a world center of art and culture. At the time Roy Lichtenstein was born to an upper-middle-class family on the bohemian Upper West Side of Manhattan, Europe, and specifically Paris, was the center of the international art world, a position solidified in the 1920s and 1930s by the Surrealist movement, led by such colorful figures as Marcel Duchamp. World War II and its aftermath would lead to a new era, one in which the United States would take Europe's place as the world leader in both geopolitics and culture. The postwar years would also spark an era of economic prosperity in the United States that transformed the culture drastically. Consumerism, commercialism, and technological innovations for the masses were the legacies of the triumph of the capitalist ideology over fascism, and these would transform society and its art.

Lichtenstein, after fighting against the Nazi threat in World War II as a soldier, would be among the vanguard of American artists who would ensure New York City's place as the most vibrant source of modern art in the latter part of the twentieth century. His artistic aspirations would be nurtured by the city's famous schools; they would be expanded by his experiences as an instructor; and they would be brought to full bloom by his eventual immersion into the thriving New York art scene—and the rapidly evolving consumer culture that drove it—in the 1950s and 1960s. Ironically, he spent a great deal of this period away from New York, but the city's hold on him was evident. By the time the seeds of Pop Art were planted, Roy Lichtenstein was home to sow them.

a CHILDHOOD OF WONDER

On October 27, 1923, Milton Lichtenstein, a German-Jewish real-estate broker originally from Brooklyn, and his wife, Beatrice (née Werner), a homemaker born in New Orleans, welcomed their first child, Roy Fox Lichtenstein, into the world at Flower Hospital (on East 64th Street, east of First Avenue).

Within a year, the family had moved from their apartment at 1457 Broadway at 96th Street to another at 305 West 86th Street, where Roy would spend his childhood years. His sister, Renée, was born in December 1927, and the children attended kindergarten near 104th Street and West End Avenue, and elementary school down the street at P.S. 9 (100 West 84th Street and West End Avenue).

Young Roy's boyhood interests pointed the way to his future vocation. He displayed an aptitude for drawing, but it took a backseat to an even stronger fascination with science, brought about by a chemistry set that he received from his parents. The two interests were destined to converge in the mechanical, methodical style of his mature work. Lichtenstein retained his interest in science throughout his life; in his later years, he was a faithful reader of *Scientific American*. His curiosity about science carried over into an interest in science fiction and fantasy; he reportedly devoured contemporary radio programs such as *Mandrake the Magician* and *Flash Gordon*—popular entertainments whose melodramatic dialogue may have found its way in some fashion into the famous word balloons on Lichtenstein's canvases years later.

As the 1920s gave way to the 1930s, several of New York's bastions of fine art were laying their foundations. The Museum of Modern Art opened in 1929 at 730 Fifth Avenue (it would relocate to 11 W. 53rd Street in 1932) with an exhibit of works by Cézanne, Gauguin, Seurat, and Van Gogh. The year 1931 saw the inaugural exhibit at the Whitney Museum of Art on West 8th Street. The Surrealist movement—spearheaded by Salvador Dali, Giorgio de Chirico, Max Ernst, and Pablo Picasso—had begun to take over the American art world, evidenced by the 1932 exhibition *Surrealisme* at the Julien Levy Gallery (602 Madison Avenue), the first major exhibition of the style in New York.

Events across the Atlantic Ocean in the 1930s were also portending changes in the art world, as Adolf Hitler's Nazi regime forced the closing of the Bauhaus in Berlin. Domestically, as the Great Depression ravaged US society, President Franklin Delano Roosevelt established the Works Project Administration/Federal Arts Project (WPA/FAP) as a New Deal relief project and a source of funding for young artistic pioneers such as Jackson Pollock and Willem de Kooning.

EMBRACING THE ARTS

In 1936, Roy Lichtenstein began eighth grade at the Franklin School for Boys, a private school at 18 West 89th Street (now the Dwight School, and relocated to Central Park West). Franklin had no art program, leaving young Lichtenstein to explore his growing interests in the arts as outside hobbies rather than vocational studies.

In addition to the visual arts, Lichtenstein developed an interest in jazz music, which was entering a golden age in New York City in the 1930s. Lichtenstein often traveled to the clubs in Harlem, such as the Apollo Theater, to sketch portraits of the musicians with their instruments.

Lichtenstein's appreciation for music—particularly classical and jazz—was evident in comments he made about his art and the artistic process in his later years. He often spoke about "building tonality" with his compositions. Asked about the significance of his *Mural with Blue Brushstroke* in 1986, Lichtenstein's characteristically enigmatic response was, "All art, good or bad, has meaning. In music like Bach or Mozart, the notes or phrases have no particular meaning. In romantic music, of course, the notes could connote waterfalls or storms." Of his bright, garish color palette, he once remarked, "I like making dissonances, like Stravinsky or Thelonious Monk."

By his early teens, Lichtenstein was as certain as he could be that he wanted to be a professional artist, and in 1937 the opportunity for formal training finally presented itself at the New York School of Fine and Applied Art, now known as Parsons School of Design (66th W. 12th Street), where Lichtenstein began attending watercolor painting classes every Saturday morning. Parsons School of Design has been a vital component of the development of

New York's artists since its founding in 1896 as the Chase School (named for the Impressionist painter William Merritt Chase) by a group of progressives who seceded from the Art Students League of New York, seeking greater individual expression. Frank Alvah Parsons, who joined the school in 1904 and soon became its president, correctly prophesied that art and design would play a vital role in the growth of industry. Toward fulfilling that promise, Parsons (the school was named after its pioneering president in 1936, six years after his death) established the first programs in the nation for fashion design, interior design, graphic design, and advertising; by the mid-1960s, the school had become firmly established as a major training ground for these industries. The middle-class American concepts of garments, furniture, living spaces, and advertisements were heavily influenced by the design professionals produced by the school. Lichtenstein's predilection toward commercial and industrial subject matter in his art—from product advertisements to the mass-produced, printed entertainment of cartoons and comics—may have taken root here on Saturday mornings.

After graduating from Franklin in June 1940, Lichtenstein was ready to pursue his art full-time. He enrolled in a painting class at the Art Students League of New York (215 W. 57th Street). Founded in 1875, and based on the atelier system of nineteenth-century France, the school boasted a roster of instructors that included William Merritt Chase, Arthur Wesley Dow, Childe Hassam, and Thomas Eakins. The alumni list is even more a who's who of American art: In addition to Lichtenstein, some of the artists who have studied their craft there are Winslow Homer, Georgia

O'Keeffe, Thomas Hart Benton, Alexander Calder, Isabel Bishop, Reginald Marsh, Jackson Pollock, Norman Rockwell, Mark Rothko, and, more recently, Chinese activist/artist Ai Weiwei. Drawing, painting, printmaking, and sculpture are the main curricula; each instructor uses his or her own views and methods, giving students a range of artistic modes, from realism to abstraction, on which to become expert.

Lichtenstein's class at the Art Students League was taught by Reginald Marsh. Born in Paris in 1898 and educated at Yale, Marsh was known as a dedicated leftist, contributing drawings to journals such as *The Unemployed*, *The Masses*, and *The Liberator*, in addition to his work as an illustrator for the *New York Daily News*. He was also celebrated for his paintings of New York, done mostly in tempera. Marsh's most well-known paintings are recognizable by their technique of applying the style of the old masters to depictions of contemporary life. Marsh also produced numerous photographs depicting contemporary life in the city in the 1930s and 1940s. Among his most frequent subjects were burlesque shows, elevated trains, movie houses, and the street life of the Bowery. Marsh's favorite place was Coney Island in Brooklyn, where the bathers on its beaches were a fertile source of anatomies, postures, and compositions for his work.

Marsh introduced Lichtenstein to model drawing and the principles of anatomy, as well as to Renaissance painting techniques and, perhaps most important, the concept of applying those techniques to the subject matter of modern life.

ONWARD TO OHIO

Lichtenstein's artistic odyssey was well under way by 1940, but, as such journeys often do, this one would take the young man on a path far away from home. Lichtenstein's parents were fairly supportive of his decision to pursue art as a career; however, they were concerned about his ability to make a decent living. They insisted their son attend a college that offered a liberal arts degree, one that would prepare him for a teaching career as a backup. In the autumn of that year, Lichtenstein left New York to begin his studies at Ohio State University, a college in Columbus that offered studio courses and a degree in fine arts. At Ohio State, Lichtenstein would encounter the instructor who he would later acknowledge had the most influence on him—Hoyt Leon Sherman, a famously eccentric professor of fine arts originally from Lafayette, Alabama.

Sherman's innovative curriculum focused on the art of seeing and perceiving objects in the mind's eye. His contention was that the mind has a tendency to misinterpret a visual stimulus because of past associations, and this philosophy had a lifelong effect on Lichtenstein, even in his latest work, such as *House I*, an optical illusion piece done in 1996.

While Lichtenstein was studying in Ohio, events were taking shape that would influence his future, both in New York and across the Atlantic Ocean in Europe. The emerging pioneers of modern art were being drawn to the Big Apple like iron filings to a magnet. The increasingly repressive atmosphere in Europe was driving many of the continent's brightest artistic stars to self-imposed exile in New York, where they were welcomed with open arms by visionary gallery owners. The presence of these artists, and their influence on their American peers, was a large factor in New York gradually usurping Paris as the artistic capital of the world. The Museum of Non-Objective Painting (later renamed the Solomon R. Guggenheim Museum) opened in May 1939 with an inaugural exhibit of works by Wassily Kandinsky, Juan Gris, Fernand Léger, and Pablo Picasso; in January 1940, the Museum of Modern Art exhibited a forty-year retrospective of Picasso's work. Piet Mondrian came to New York in 1940, and Max Ernst arrived in 1941, marrying Peggy Guggenheim in December of that year. Marcel Duchamp, who roomed with Ernst for a short time in 1942, set up shop in a studio/residence at 210 West 14th Street in 1943. In fall 1942, the Reid Mansion (451 Madison Avenue) hosted the *First Papers of Surrealism* exhibit, showcasing the works of Jean Arp, William Bazoles, Alexander Calder, Robert Motherwell, Paul Klee, Joan Miró, Ernst, Picasso, and others. The highlight of the groundbreaking show was *16 Miles of String*, an enormous, weblike construction by Duchamp that filled the hall. Contemporary art was moving inexorably toward radically modernized areas that would reach new heights in the work of Jackson Pollock, Willem de Kooning, Jasper Johns, and, eventually, Lichtenstein, Warhol, and other Pop artists.

LIFE DURING WARTIME

While a generation of artists was marching into the galleries of Manhattan, the jackbooted troops of Hitler's Nazi

Hoyt Sherman and the Science of Aesthetics

One of the signature artistic exercises that Hoyt Sherman employed with his students at Ohio State University in the 1940s and 1950s was known as the "flash room." In this exercise, students sat in a darkened room with their sketchbooks while a slide of an abstract drawing flashed across a large screen for a brief instant. Students attempted to mentally grasp the image and reproduce it from memory in the dark, copying it as accurately as possible. One of Lichtenstein's most well-known paintings, *I Can See the Whole Room—And There's Nobody in It!*, with its depiction of two scientists peeking through a hole surrounded by blackness, almost reminiscent of a camera's shutter opening to let in light to capture the image, may be a nod to Sherman's flash room teachings. "You'd get a very strong afterimage," Lichtenstein later said of the exercise,

> and then you'd draw in the dark, the point being that you'd have to sense where the parts were in relation to the whole. It was a mixture of science and aesthetics, and it became the center of what I was interested in. Sherman was hard to understand, but he taught that the key to everything lay in what he called perceptual unity.

Other means Sherman employed to teach this lesson included turning familiar objects usually seen from only one angle—such as tables and chairs—upside down or suspending them from ceilings, so pupils could perceive them from new perspectives and represent them as objects in space. Sherman published several handbooks and manuals that Lichtenstein later owned, including *Cézanne and Visual Form* (1952), in which Sherman studied (and praised) Cézanne's compositions for their adjustment of elements, independent of reality, for the sake of visual unity. (Years later, these books would provide the inspiration for Lichtenstein's series of paintings based on Cézanne's work.) Modern art, according to Sherman, came of age when artists, starting with Cézanne, began to abandon the customary one-point perspective in favor of overlapping planes to convey distance—more in tune with how the human mind and eye perceive space. This design principle is one that can be found in nearly all the "comic book" paintings from Lichtenstein's early 1960s period.

Germany were marching across Western Europe. In 1941, with debate raging in the United States over whether to intervene in World War II, the Japanese launched an early-morning sneak attack on the US naval base at Pearl Harbor, Hawaii, that galvanized the nation. Hitler himself ultimately settled the question a few days later, declaring war on the United States. Swept into the struggle by the maelstrom of history, America came to Europe's aid, and the early 1940s were largely defined by the struggle against Nazism, just as the 1930s had been defined by the Great Depression. Young men—whether they were laborers, doctors, engineers, or even aspiring artists—were expected to serve their country on the battlefields of France, Germany, Italy, and North Africa.

In Ohio in February 1943, Roy Lichtenstein received his draft notice from the US Army. His college education interrupted and his artistic aspirations put on hold, he left Ohio State for Fort Dix, New Jersey, where he was inducted. In March, he reported to Camp Hulen, Texas, for his basic training. Located on the shore of Lake Matagorda, two miles from the town of Palacios, Hulen was an antiaircraft training center that was legendary for taking raw recruits from all over the country and molding them into well-trained fighting units. Lichtenstein showed promise as a fighter pilot. By the winter of 1943, he was sent to DePaul University in Chicago, where he entered the army's ASTP (Army Special Training Program) for engineering. He took two semesters of math and science courses before the army canceled the program. Lichtenstein still seemed headed for a military career as a pilot when he arrived at Keesler Air Force Base in Biloxi, Mississippi, in 1944. Those plans were derailed, however, when one of the most costly battles of the war necessitated the cancellation of the pilot training program.

The Battle of the Bulge took place in the Ardennes Forest on the German-Belgian border in some of the most brutally cold, snowy conditions of the entire war. Fighting started on December 16, 1944, and didn't end until January 25, 1945. The conflict involved more than a million soldiers from Germany, America, and Britain. The number of casualties was staggering on all sides, and America found itself with an immediate need for active-duty infantrymen to replace the enormous number of soldiers killed. Thus did Lichtenstein—art student, engineering whiz, and aspiring flyboy—find himself among the grunts of the engineer battalion of the "Fighting 69th" Infantry Division, shipping out to Europe in December 1944 and stationed in France a mile from the front by January 1945.

The 69th Infantry Division of the 9th Army entered the European Theater of Operations in 1945, seeing combat in France, Belgium, and the Rhineland throughout the opening months of 1945; by late April, the division had participated in the liberation of Leipzig-Thekla, a subcamp of the infamous Buchenwald concentration camp. When he wasn't involved in combat operations, Lichtenstein spent his quiet time with his sketchbooks, drawing landscapes of the foreign lands he saw on his tour of duty and portraits of soldiers in his division—two of whom, Ellsworth Kelly and Richard Artswager, would also become major artists. In an interesting bit of symmetry, a comics illustrator named Irving Novick, whose work for DC Comics in the 1960s was among the "source material" for some of Lichtenstein's works, was also assigned to the unit. In an interview years later, Novick claimed that he was Lichtenstein's superior officer for a time, and even helped him in his artistic development by giving him military posters and signs to design. Many people have disputed this account, however, pointing out that Novick says that he first encountered Lichtenstein in 1947, after Lichtenstein had left the army.

Whether the story is outright false or Novick's memory for dates was simply faulty, critics of Lichtenstein's art have seized upon the apparent irony that Novick, who apparently helped Lichtenstein pursue his artistic vocation, was, in their minds, unjustly ignored as an inspiration. Alastair Sooke, writing for the BBC in 2014, noted, "After spotting Lichtenstein's talent as a draughtsman, Novick took him off latrine-mopping duty and got him designing signs and posters instead." Fifteen years later, Novick was drawing war comic books for DC Comics in New York, and Lichtenstein was using some of them as sources for his paintings, notably *Whaam!* and *Okay, Hot Shot* (1963).

On May 8, 1945, VE Day, Germany surrendered unconditionally to the Western Allies and the Soviet Union. Three months later, on August 15, Japan surrendered after atomic bombs were dropped on the cities of Hiroshima and Nagasaki, officially ending World War II while at the same time ushering in a frightening new age.

In October, Lichtenstein found himself in Paris, attending a French Language and Civilization course at the Sorbonne. He would return to the United States by early December, however, upon learning that his father, Milton, was gravely ill. He was furloughed back to the United States to spend time with his father, and by the end of 1945, he was back in New Jersey at Fort Dix.

Milton Lichtenstein passed away in January 1946, and his son was honorably discharged from the US Army as Private First Class, with a medal for meritorious service. For Roy, however, the time was not right to move back to the New York area. After his father's funeral, he returned to Ohio State to complete his bachelor of fine arts degree on the GI Bill. He received his diploma in June, and entered the graduate program that fall; he also taught art classes there. During the years that he was ensconced in the Midwest, Lichtenstein would begin to produce his first paintings, in styles that today's admirers of his work would not even recognize—paintings influenced heavily by the European modernism of Paul Klee and Pablo Picasso, and dealing with subjects similar to those in nineteenth-century American genre painting. It would take the artist several years—and a lot of time studying the work in New York's galleries—to catch up to the rapidly evolving trends in American art.

THE AGE OF THE ACTION PAINTING

The years immediately following World War II were significant in the art world, especially for New York City, as it was during this time that New York supplanted Paris as the recognized center of the art world. The first significant sign of the regime change was an article in the March 30, 1946, edition of the *New Yorker*, in which critic Robert Coates coined the term "Abstract Expressionism" to describe the works of three emerging artists, all of whom worked in New York: Jackson Pollock, Willem de Kooning, and Arshile Gorky. Initially referred to as "the New York school," this group of pioneers and others who would soon follow played a major role in establishing New York as the epicenter of modern American painting. Abstract Expressionism was seen as an artistic movement that combined the deeply personal, emotional intensity of the Expressionists (such as Edvard Munch, Franz Marc, Ernst Ludwig Kirchner, and Kandinsky) with the antifigurative tendencies of European schools, such as Cubism, Futurism, and the Bauhaus style.

Abstract Expressionism and the CIA

How seriously did the US government take the communist threat during the early years of the Cold War? Seriously enough to thrust its influence into the world of American art. In March 1949, the Waldorf Astoria in New York hosted a peace conference in which the day's most prominent pacifists made a case for peace with Stalin's Soviet Union. It was in response to this meeting, many believe, that the Congress for Cultural Freedom (CCF), an anticommunist advocacy group, was founded. Established at the Titania Palace in democratic West Berlin in June 1950, the CCF's stated goal was to disprove the growing notion among intellectuals that "bourgeois democracy" was incompatible with high culture.

In Abstract Expressionism, the CCF found the perfect vehicle to spread its message that the democratic, free-market system of the United States was a haven for free thought and expression and that American art was destined to prevail over the socialist realism that still dominated European art. To this end, the CCF—eventually renamed the International Association for Cultural Freedom (IACF)—provided funding and promotion for artists such as Pollock throughout the 1950s. What might have amazed the artists, however, was the revelation in 1966 that the CCF/IACF was funded by the Central Intelligence Agency (CIA), part of a larger network of anticommunist cultural groups in thirty-five countries intended to sway the support of Soviet-sympathizing liberals around the world.

Abstract Expressionism, as typified by the Action Painting of Pollock, was seen as energetic, rebellious, anarchistic, and distinctly American—the first American art movement, in fact, to gain international acclaim. The Abstract Expressionists demonstrated to many art critics throughout the world that the United States was breaking away from European standards of artistic beauty and forging its own identity. Like the United States itself, Abstract Expressionism was seen by Europeans—and, initially, by many critics at home—as brash, boastful, and rebellious, with its spontaneity of style, massive scale, and deliberate disdain for established European traditions. To a nation that had claimed its position as a superpower by once again turning the tide in a European war, this was a major cultural development. As the Cold War with the Soviet Union cast its frosty, meanicng shadow over the following decades, the notion of the United States as a haven of free creative thought was more important than ever.

Pop Art has been seen by both its staunchest defenders and its most vociferous critics as a rebellion against Abstract Expressionism—the ultrarealism and emphasis on mass-market culture of the former an apparent rejoinder to the splashed colors and nonrepresentational forms of the latter. But it was Abstract Expressionism that ushered in the rebellious, free-thinking mindset—the broadening of what could be seen and described legitimately as art—and that made the Pop Art movement possible. Lichtenstein, for his own part, traveled the path from the former to the latter in a very methodical, deliberate way.

In 1947, Lichtenstein took his first tentative steps back to his New York roots by visiting New York art galleries, where he began to discover the radically different art that would exert its influence on his next decade's worth of work. His regular stops included the Charles Egan Gallery, which had exhibited the paintings of New York artist Robert De Niro Sr. (father of the Academy Award–winning actor), and the Betty Parsons Gallery (15 E. 57th Street). Betty Parsons was one of New York's first important gallery owners, with a dedication to showcasing new and exciting styles. Born into wealth in 1900, the native New Yorker dedicated her life to seeking out what she considered "new" art after being profoundly influenced as a child by the groundbreaking work at the city's 1913 Armory Show. Her own experiences as an outsider may have played a role in this mission. A closeted lesbian who was a friend of writer Gertrude Stein—and who allegedly had a flirtation with reclusive actress Greta Garbo—Parsons opened her gallery in Manhattan in 1946 after several years in Paris and Southern California. Although the censorious excesses of the McCarthyite 1950s made it prudent for Parsons to be intensely private about her sexuality, she nevertheless became known for supporting the art of gay and lesbian artists such as Ellsworth Kelly. She was the first to exhibit the work of Robert Rauschenberg, along with that of Jasper Johns, one of Lichtenstein's most prominent Pop Art influences. Gay or straight, however, if the art was new and challenging, Betty Parsons (whose gallery became one of the most prestigious in the city before it closed in 1981, one year before her death) was interested in showing it. Hers was one of the first galleries to give significant exposure to the mostly staunch heterosexuals of the Abstract Expressionist movement, epitomized by Pollock and de Kooning.

LOVE IN OHIO, CHANGES IN NEW YORK

Lichtenstein's work in this phase of his career consisted of American genre paintings, all influenced by the Cubist and Expressionist style of artists such as Picasso, whom he obviously admired. Throughout the later 1940s, Lichtenstein tried his hand at various styles and assorted media. He painted in oils and pastels, and also produced drawings. His subject matter ranged from landscapes and musicians to fantasy and fairy tales, with visual nods to *Alice in Wonderland* and *Beauty and the Beast*. Lichtenstein's trips to the New York galleries were educational, and he was slowly becoming aware that the art scene in America was changing, becoming even more vibrant and experimental and more welcoming to wildly divergent styles, as evidenced by more major figures converging on New York (Jasper Johns arrived in 1949) and the media beginning to take notice of the shifting trends.

The *Partisan Review* published an article by influential American art critic Clement Greenberg in 1948 called "The Decline of Cubism," pronouncing confidently that American art had broken with the School of Paris and attained supremacy. Greenberg was a major proponent of avantgarde, Modernist art, especially Abstract Expressionism, which he saw as a response to what he deemed the "dumbing down" of culture due to consumerism. Greenberg used a now-ubiquitous term for the phenomenon: "kitsch." (As one might expect, his reaction to Pop Art—which for him, was the very definition of kitsch—was not nearly as positive as his response to Abstract Expressionism.) But it was not just the learned critics such as Greenberg who were enthralled by what they were seeing in the galleries of Manhattan. By 1949, the work of Pollock, widely derided when it first burst on the scene earlier in the decade, had the critics at *Life* magazine famously asking, "Is He the Greatest Living Painter in the US?" The article would have a sequel of sorts in *Life*'s January 31, 1964, issue devoted to Lichtenstein.

Lichtenstein had one New York milestone in 1949—his first group exhibition, at the Chinese Gallery (formerly located at 38 E. 57th Street, now an office building). For a young artist trying to make the New York scene, it was a breakthrough, though the lukewarm critical reaction to his work may have been one reason he wasn't ready to take the plunge into full-time painting just yet.

Lichtenstein was setting down roots in his adopted Midwestern home. While finishing his graduate studies at Ohio State, he had made the acquaintance of the codirector of the Ten-Thirty Gallery in Cleveland, an Ohio farm girl named Isabel Wilson Saritsky, and in 1949 they were married. That year, he also received his MFA and moved to a new residence within Columbus. The marriage to Isabel would ensure that Lichtenstein remained in Ohio as the new decade dawned.

Although he was placing distance physically between himself and the city of his birth, Roy Lichtenstein's bond with New York—and his determination to prove himself as an artist there—would only grow stronger in the coming decade.

3

THIS IS TOMORROW

A CHANGING OF THE GUARD

World War II and its aftermath ushered in a sea change in American culture. The prosperity and enhanced world prestige that resulted from the United States' instrumental role in the defeat of Nazism and fascism brought about the rise of a consumer culture, which affected the lives of every American. The midpoint of the postwar decade, 1955, brought the opening of both Disneyland and McDonald's, and John F. Kennedy, elected in 1960, is regarded as the first chief executive to fully exploit the power of television, which was rapidly becoming a necessity, rather than a luxury, in America's living rooms. Art in America was destined to get swept up in this culture and to respond to it in ways that were widely different from anything that had ever before been seen. The pure, nonobjective emotion of Abstract Expressionism was on the verge of being rendered passé by work that embraced the country's inexorable shift into technology and commercialism—the experimental melodies of composer John Cage, which inspired the Happenings of Allan Kaprow, which in turn gave birth to what is today known as Pop Art. The eye of this revolutionary cultural storm was New York City.

Lisa Phillips, in *The American Century*, sums up the prevailing social movement nicely:

> As Kennedy understood, the power and influence of the media were here to stay. The media fed the consumer culture through advertising and the promotion of a lifestyle that encouraged spending on both necessities and luxuries. By 1960, the acquisition of manufactured goods was becoming a national pastime. Television sets and cars joined apple pie and the flag as quintessential symbols of America. The culture of consumption had begun to transform America drastically in the Fifties. . . . A new shampoo could bring you romance, a new laundry detergent a happier home, and a new brand of cigarettes greater virility. . . . The imagery of advertising had become so pervasive—so invasive—that it was an essential feature of American life and identity.

Truly, it was only a matter of time before artists, always a barometer of the cultural zeitgeist, would discover inspiration in their new, commercialized world—even if one of the most important artists still needed to find his way home from the quiet confines of Midwestern academia.

ODD JOBS and EARLY ART

The 1950s began with the newlywed Lichtensteins moving from their home on 15th Avenue in Columbus to a new residence on Perry Street, and with Roy embarking on a series of short-lived jobs, many of which were decidedly pedestrian for a graduate with an MFA degree. He taught drawing at the Cooper School, a commercial-arts institution. He worked as an engineering draftsman at Republic Steel, and at a part-time position decorating windows at Halle Brothers department store. Lichtenstein designed black-and-white dials for the Hickok Electrical Instrument Company, and made project models for a local architectural firm. One can begin to see how these jobs—and the drudgery of applying a fine-art sensibility to commercial, consumerist endeavors—may have helped plant the seed for the groundbreaking work that was to come a few years hence.

However, Lichtenstein's personal artistic pursuits were still rooted in the Modernist styles of Picasso and, to an extent, Paul Klee. The paintings he produced in the early 1950s were centered around distinctly American themes, notably cowboys and Indians of the Wild West, and historical tableaux, including his version of *Washington Crossing the Delaware* (1951).

Lichtenstein's visits to New York became more frequent during the 1950s, and the work he was seeing in the galleries was beginning to have an influence on his own. Although he had not yet taken the quantum leap that defined his legacy in the 1960s, the paintings and sculptures he produced in this era bear more evidence of creative risk-taking than their predecessors. The year 1951 was a breakthrough year for Lichtenstein as an exhibiting New York artist, although his mature style was still nearly a decade away from being fully developed.

With his paintings strapped to the top of his station wagon, Lichtenstein regularly drove hundreds of miles from Ohio to New York City, peddling the work to some of the hottest galleries of the time, notably M. Knoedler and Sidney Janis. The visits began to bear some fruit in March 1951, when his woodcut work, *To Battle*, was exhibited in the *Fifth National Print Annual Exhibition*, a juried show of over two hundred artists at the Brooklyn Museum (200 Eastern Parkway). The work was one of only twenty selected to receive the museum's Purchase Award and become part of the museum's collection.

Lichtenstein broke into the Manhattan scene with his first solo exhibition at the Carlebach Gallery (937 Third Avenue). By this point, he was also trying his hand at odd, avant-garde sculptural pieces, inspired by the bric-a-brac of his engineering jobs. Critic Larry Campbell, in the May 1951 issue of *ARTNews*, gave the Carlebach show a fairly positive review, saying,

> Roy Lichtenstein . . . recognizes the faces that appear on buttons and electric light outlets and ushers them with mock ceremony into the inner sanctum—a half-naïve, private world of dots, hooks, eyes, pegs, little jagged shapes, like torn paper, and things that look like bow ties, all in muted pinks, blues and mauves. From this completely ingenuous way of looking at things, it is a short

step to the concoction of *TheWarrior* from a file and a pink drill-buffer, and *The Horse* from a lump of wood, a handle for opening a window, and an absurd screw.

Campbell summed up his reaction to the exhibition thusly: "His first one-man show reveals a curious and amusing mind in the act of discovering a personal syntax of form."

If Roy Lichtenstein was beginning to become a known commodity on the New York art scene in the 1950s, he had not yet found a place among his peers, despite making himself an infrequent visitor to one of their most legendary gathering places, the Cedar Tavern. Lichtenstein had heard about the Cedar from two friends in Ohio, Herman Cherry and Warren Brandt, and began to make stops there on his increasingly frequent jaunts to Manhattan. However, his natural shyness prevented him from getting to know the giants of Abstract Expressionism.

The Cedar Tavern, on University Place in Greenwich Village, a short walk from the heart of New York University, was a regular hangout for the New York artists' community and was frequented by Pollock, de Kooning, Rothko, Franz Kline, and Robert Motherwell, all in their still semi-starving-artist days. The original Cedar was the successor to "the Club," an informal gathering spot in a rented loft (39 East 8th Street), and stood in the heart of New York's midcentury "Boho Belt," which also included the storied Brevier Hotel, home to Isadora Duncan and Edna St. Vincent Millay. It relocated to 82 University Place, between 11th and 12th Streets, a few blocks up from its original site, in the 1960s. Many stories and legends have sprung up from those days at the Cedar, such as the alcohol-fueled dramas between de Kooning and his wife, artist Elaine Fried. Pollock was once banned from the tavern after ripping the men's room door off its hinges in a drunken rage. Another famous patron, Beat generation writer Jack Kerouac, was once supposedly tossed from the bar for urinating in an ashtray. Despite the occasional outbursts of violence and pathos, the Cedar Tavern, with its rustic decor of oak and brass, touches of stained glass, and almost perpetually dark atmosphere, proved a haven for these artists, a shelter from a skeptical world that had yet to fully embrace them.

Perhaps it's just as well that Lichtenstein didn't engage with the old guard at the tavern, considering the reception that Andy Warhol got when he first walked into the Cedar in the 1960s. Warhol took just a few steps through the door; his white hair and effeminate bearing stupefied the gathered crowd of Abstract Expressionists (de Kooning reportedly their ringleader), moving one of them to grab Warhol by the hair and jacket and physically toss him back out the door—to the thunderous acclaim of the others. It was a symbolic moment for the two schools of art—one, Abstract Expressionism, forcibly rejecting the incursion of the other, Pop Art, into the spotlight they had considered theirs alone. Warhol and the Pop artists would have the last laugh, of course, as their work would largely supplant that of their predecessors in the cultural mindset by the end of the 1950s.

Lichtenstein's other solo exhibition in 1951 was at the John Heller Gallery (108 E. 57th Street); Americana and frontier themes were still prevalent in his painted work.

The Heller Gallery show's brochure features a preface by Lichtenstein's drawing mentor, Hoyt Sherman, and one of the paintings, a historical military piece called *Death of the General*, was reproduced in two of the leading art magazines, *ARTNews* and *Art Digest*. Also garnering some attention were several self-portraits of the artist as a medieval knight, significant because from that point on, Lichtenstein would rarely make himself the subject of his art.

Lichtenstein was denied tenure at Ohio State in the summer of 1951. When Isabel found work as a decorator in Cleveland, the couple moved there. In March 1952, the Art Colony Galleries in Cleveland hosted a solo exhibition of Lichtenstein's work, featuring a variety of paintings, prints, and drawings. The review of the show by the art critic of the *Cleveland News* gives a taste of what was to come at the beginning of the Pop Art era. One of the pencil drawings, *Knight Storming Castle*, included a photograph of a castle taped to the drawing as a collage element, prompting the critic to describe the work as "truly like the doodling of a five-year-old." It would not be the last time Lichtenstein's artistic maturity would be questioned by the art world's intelligentsia.

Perhaps if the show had taken place in a New York gallery, with a New York audience, the critical reaction would have been different—but judging from the harsh responses to the artist's early Pop works by the city's ostensibly sophisticated critics, it is hard to say so with certainty. Nevertheless, by the end of 1952, Lichtenstein's work had become sufficiently well known—and perhaps, sufficiently controversial—to be shown in juried exhibitions at the

Denver Art Museum, the University of Nebraska, the Pennsylvania Academy of Fine Arts, and New York's Metropolitan Museum of Art.

In New York, Abstract Expressionism was still king, and thanks to critic Harold Rosenberg writing in the December 1952 issue of *ARTNews*, the kinetic, splatter-filled canvases of Pollock and others now had a name: Action Painting. Rosenberg considered this style "the most vigorous and original movement in art in the history of the nation." The unqualified praise by one of the era's most revered art commentators had a profound effect on New York's—and hence America's—artistic landscape.

Rosenberg's analysis of the style, in contrast to Clement Greenberg's, focused on the act of painting itself, rather than the result on the canvas. Behind the splattered and caked-on gobs of oil paint, the viewer was supposed to recognize an existential struggle. By introducing psychoanalysis into art, Rosenberg was further redefining what art could be—inspiring the wild experimentation of Allan Kaprow's Happenings and thus, indirectly, the art of Lichtenstein.

Lichtenstein's paintings, both oils and watercolors, were still largely based on Americana themes, and many were on display at his second solo exhibit at the John Heller Gallery in January and February 1953. A little more than a year later, at his third solo show at the Heller Gallery, the subject matter of Lichtenstein's paintings was beginning to expand in scope. The familiar folklore themes were still there, but now they were joined by different types of imagery, featuring artistic renderings of machine parts based on engineers' blueprints. Lichtenstein's engineering design background was becoming evident in his painting, and it was just one of the precursors to the hard-edged, meticulously designed style that would come to define his work. Throughout the next few years, more hints of Lichtenstein's 1960s style would begin to emerge, with titles and advertising copy finding their way into some of his paintings and woodcut compositions.

Art critic Fairfield Porter noted the childlike qualities of these new works. "Roy Lichtenstein's paintings are not about beauty, either negatively or positively," he commented in the March 1954 issue of *ARTNews*.

> If twenty years ago paintings like his had been made, it would have been difficult to find an audience. . . . He paints a version of an American historical painting as reproduced in a grammar school textbook . . . and lately, versions of engineers' blueprints of machine details, assemblies, and sub-assemblies from his experience as a mechanical draftsman. His life as a schoolboy, soldier, and teacher of art are all in his paintings . . . he retains in his adulthood the child's way of using things, including his own toys (for instance, his art) for purposes for which they were not intended. He is like an observant child who finds the grown-up conversation very funny.

Lichtenstein once reminisced about those lean days in Cleveland. "I was taking the stodgy pictures you see in history textbooks and doing them in a modern art way. . . . It was making a comment on other people's graphic work, which I'm still doing, and it was ironic, though not ironic enough, I guess."

TransiTionaL arT

While Roy Lichtenstein was making ends meet in Ohio with odd jobs and the occasional sale of his work, another struggling artist was doing the same in New York. Jasper Johns was born in 1930 in Augusta, Georgia, and attended the University of South Carolina and Parsons School of Design. By 1954, he was living in a loft on Pearl Street in downtown Manhattan, where he produced the painting that is widely seen as the prototype of what would come to be known as Pop Art. The simply titled *Flag* was inspired by a dream that Johns had about the American flag, and applies the rich, feathery brushstrokes of Abstract Expressionism—a defiantly nonrepresentational style—to a famously representational subject. *Flag*, which would inspire an entire series of such paintings, was included in Johns's first solo exhibit at the Leo Castelli Gallery, the same gallery that would be instrumental in the careers of Lichtenstein and his Pop Art contemporaries in the sixties.

At the time that he painted his first *Flag*, Johns was working on window displays at New York department stores such as Tiffany and Bonwit Teller along with a fellow transplanted Southern artist, Robert Rauschenberg from Port Arthur, Texas. By 1955, Johns and Rauschenberg were living in the same building and had become lovers as well as artistic peers, regularly seeing and critiquing each other's work. While Johns was creating his *Flag* series, and later his *Target* series and number paintings, Rauschenberg was breaking ground of his own with his mixed-collage "combines." Both men rejected what they perceived as the seriousness and angst of Abstract Expressionism while they appreciated the energetic painting technique the style employed.

By reintroducing figurative subject matter into American art, Johns and Rauschenberg—specifically in their seminal works in the 1950s—were the transitional figures between Abstract Expressionism and Pop Art. The backlash against the hegemony of Action Painting had begun, and Lichtenstein—along with Warhol, Tom Wesselman, Dine, Claes Oldenburg, and other young mavericks champing at the bit in their modest New York studios—was soon to take up the gauntlet.

Lichtenstein's personal milestone in 1954 was the birth of his first child, David Hoyt, on October 9. As it turned out, this new addition to the family, along with the birth of his second child, Mitchell Wilson, on March 10, 1956, would soon lead to a career milestone as well—for what father of two young boys is not inevitably slated to come into contact with popular children's entertainments, such as cartoon characters and comic book heroes?

Throughout 1955, while Johns and Rauschenberg were creating their works (dubbed neo-Dada by some critics), Lichtenstein was achieving a modest level of financial success in Ohio. A historical painting, *The Surrender of Weatherford to Jackson*, became the first of several of his works to be purchased for the permanent collection of the Butler Museum of American Art in Youngstown. Thirteen of his paintings were displayed as part of a three-person show at the Art Colony Galleries, with the repertoire once again encompassing both American folklore themes—such as *Indians*—and more of his modern, mechanically themed subjects that drew upon his engineering draftsman work, such as *A Flying Device* and *Perpetual Motion Machine*. The overall effect, according to one critic, was "Klee-like and surprising."

It is a lithograph, however, rather than a painting, that is regarded as Lichtenstein's first "proto-Pop" work. *Ten Dollar Bill*, created in 1956 in an edition of twenty-five, may have been influenced by Johns's *Flag* series, but the former's jovial, cartoonish style was a departure from the painterly motif of the latter. With this, the true progenitor of Lichtenstein's most successful artistic period, one might have expected that the work done subsequent to it would continue in that vein. However, it would be nearly five years before Lichtenstein would take the next stylistic step toward his mature style.

The still-struggling artist tried his hand at Abstract Expressionism, perhaps for reasons of sheer practicality and economics—it was the reigning artistic school in America in the latter half of the 1950s, and it was in demand by most of the best galleries in New York. Lichtenstein at the time may have had no idea what turns his artistic fortunes would take, but he knew that he was determined to get back to the artistic promised land, New York.

enDInGS anD BeGInnInGS

In what was perhaps the beginning of the end for the age of Abstract Expressionism, Jackson Pollock was killed in an alcohol-related automobile accident near his home in Long Island, New York, on August 11, 1956, cutting short his meteoric career at the relatively young age of forty-four. Lichtenstein was thirty-three when he began his own foray into the Abstract Expressionist style, a relative latecomer who had not received widespread acclaim or discovered a truly personal style.

On February 1, 1957, another significant event helped paved the way for a changing of the artistic guard in America: Leo Castelli opened his eponymous art gallery on 4 East 77th Street in New York. The inaugural exhibit showcased a roster of stars such as Pollock, de Kooning, Alberto Giacometti, and Kandinsky. Despite the preponderance of Abstract Expressionism exhibited there in its early days, Castelli's gallery would emerge as one of the primary launching pads for the Pop Art movement—and for the career of Roy Lichtenstein.

In January of that same year, he had his final solo show at the Heller Gallery, consisting of more Americana-themed paintings. With a growing family to support, and still not having found major financial success as a full-time fine artist, Lichtenstein returned to the world of teaching, accepting a position as assistant professor of art at the State University of New York at Oswego. In the summer of 1957, after nearly a decade in Ohio, Lichtenstein, Isabel, and their two sons packed up and moved to the picturesque country town on the shores of Lake Ontario, a nearly five-hour drive from the bright lights and excitement of New York City.

The 1960s were looming, and New York and the rest of America were on the verge of one of the most turbulent decades in their history. For Lichtenstein, now approaching the age of forty and only a marginally successful artist, the decade would also bring levels of success—and controversy—that he had never imagined.

4

a Happening Time

GOTHAM PUSHES THE ARTISTIC ENVELOPE

The late 1950s and early 1960s proved to be the turning point in the career of Roy Lichtenstein. They were also years that witnessed era-defining political and cultural developments both at home and abroad.

The Soviet Union launched its first orbiting space satellites, *Sputnik I* and *Sputnik II*, in 1957, officially kicking off the space race and raising the stakes in the escalating Cold War. NASA was established the following year and released its first satellite. America wanted to be the first to reach the moon in order to prove its technological superiority to the Soviet Union, and this mindset permeated not only government policy but also mass culture and entertainment. John F. Kennedy and his elegant, photogenic first lady,

Jacqueline, brought a sense of optimism and adventure to the country, especially its youth. Kennedy spurred the US space program, and in 1962, a Marine Corps pilot-turned-astronaut named John Glenn became the first American to orbit the Earth.

Meanwhile, a youth counterculture like none seen before in the country was bubbling to the surface, fed by the writings of Jack Kerouac, the songs of Bob Dylan, and the canvases of artists such as Jasper Johns and Robert Rauschenberg. Across the globe, momentous cultural and political events were setting the stage for the turbulent sixties: the building of the Berlin Wall, the Cuban missile crisis, America's entry into Vietnam, and what many consider the tipping point, the assassination of President Kennedy before the end of his first term.

In New York City, the innocence and enthusiasm of the 1950s was only slowly giving way to a more questioning mood. In 1958, the leading musical on Broadway was *The Sound of Music*. In 1959, the Guggenheim Museum opened in its current Frank Lloyd Wright–designed home on the Upper East Side. The new Cuban dictator, Fidel Castro, paid a visit to the city in 1960. The New York Mets, the city's long-awaited new National League baseball team, had their inaugural season in 1962, setting a Major League Baseball record for losses (120 games), which had fans lamenting even more the defection of Brooklyn's beloved Dodgers to Los Angeles several years before. By the end of the decade, everything would be turned on its ear: *Hair* would be the must-see musical, the Mets would be champions, and the city would be embroiled in massive social change.

This era marked Roy Lichtenstein's turning point as well, as he found his way back to New York and discovered the people, places, and events that gave him the courage to abandon Picasso-esque Modernism and half-hearted Action Painting and to create the art that only he could—art that hit the Manhattan scene with a resounding *blam!*

Galleries Support New Art

By 1958, the writing was on the wall for the end of Abstract Expressionism's reign over the art world—or perhaps a better metaphor might be that the painting was on the wall. On January 20, New York art lovers got their first good look at the work of Jasper Johns at his first solo exhibition at the Leo Castelli Gallery. Johns's work *Target with Four Faces* was reproduced on the cover of *ARTNews* magazine's January 1958 issue. Another of the exhibit's featured paintings was *Alley Oop*, a collage work that included a panel from the Vincent Hamlin comic strip of the same name. The 1930s cartoon character would not be the last to grace the walls of New York's galleries over the next few years. Even if Lichtenstein saw this exhibit, however—or the mixed-media piece *Dublin* (1959) by West Coast artist Edward Ruscha, which incorporates portions of the *Little Orphan Annie* strip—it seems to have had little influence on his own art at the time.

In Oswego, when he wasn't teaching art classes, Lichtenstein was working on untitled Abstract Expressionist paintings, his previous efforts with American genre

Pop Prototypes in London

New York City was undeniably the epicenter of the Pop Art movement, but most art historians agree that an exhibition across the pond in London, England, was its true launching pad. *This Is Tomorrow* was the lofty-sounding name of the show, held in 1956 at the Whitechapel Art Gallery in London, which is widely seen as pioneering the Pop Art style through the works of an informally affiliated group of artists known as the Independent Group (or IG). The group included architects, painters, sculptors, and art critics who focused on the popular mass culture of the United States as the inspiration for their work.

The most famous name exhibited at the show was the painter Richard Hamilton, a London native who is regarded in some circles as the true father of Pop Art. Furthermore, it is Hamilton's groundbreaking collage piece with an unwieldy title, *Just What Is It That Makes Today's Homes So Different, So Appealing?*, that is widely described as the first work of Pop. The eye-catching work used clippings from American magazines in a mélange that Hamilton used to sum up Yankee culture: a beefcake husband from a bodybuilding ad (holding a giant Tootsie Pop); a blonde stripper housewife; a canned ham on an end table; a cover of the *Young Romance* comic book on the wall of the ideal upper-middle-class home. It was an image that struck right at the heart of the growing fascination the Brits had with postwar America, with all its prepackaged, mass-produced, glamorous, sexy splendor.

Other members of the IG who were represented at *This Is Tomorrow* were painters Eduardo Paolozzi and Magda Cordell, photographer Nigel Henderson, architects Alison and Peter Smithson, and the art critic Lawrence Alloway, who would go on to write extensively about Pop Art, and Lichtenstein, throughout the 1960s. The Smithsons also made a prophetic statement at the time, writing, "Advertising has caused a revolution in the popular art field. Advertising has become respectable in its own right and is beating the fine arts at their old game . . . [and] making a bigger contribution to our visual climate than any of the traditional fine arts." Even the Smithsons, however, probably had no idea how big that contribution would be in the next decade in the United States.

Britain, like the United States, was poised for major social and cultural changes as the 1960s dawned. The halcyon days of "Swinging London" were looming, and the emergence of British Pop Art was a harbinger of the musical British Invasion that would have such a profound effect on American youth in that dynamic decade. Ultimately, however, it would be the Americans—specifically the ones who'd gathered in New York in the late 1950s, led by Lichtenstein, Warhol, and others—who took the reins of this trend in art. Although the British were fascinated with US consumer culture, it seemed that only those living close to its heart could fully grasp what it meant, and could so effectively capture the cultural zeitgeist that was radically transforming their nation throughout the 1950s and 1960s.

painting having largely failed to bring the New York native any great level of financial or critical success. If he was aware of the shift that was slowly taking place in the art world at the end of the 1950s, Lichtenstein seemed determined to ignore it. More likely, his distance from New York City and the galleries where the transition was occurring account for Lichtenstein's tardy arrival on the stage for Abstract Expressionism's final act. So fertile and fast-changing was the art scene in the Big Apple that an artist who was sequestered even a few hours away was hard-pressed to keep up. Fortunately for Lichtenstein, his life was on the verge of major change.

Lichtenstein's contemporaries, meanwhile, were settling into place for Pop Art's opening curtain in New York. James Rosenquist was employed as a billboard painter for Artkraft Strauss, and Jim Dine had been helping to stage Happenings in New York since moving to the city in 1958 after graduating from Ohio University. In London, Lawrence Alloway—who had been an instrumental part of the Whitechapel Gallery show in 1956—authored an article in *Architectural Digest* called "The Arts and the Mass Media." The article included the first use of the phrase "popular art." Alloway would spill a large amount of ink on the analysis of such art in the coming years.

The Leo Castelli Gallery continued to provide an outlet for the emerging style that was beginning to supplant Abstract Expressionism. In addition to showcasing the work of Johns that year, Castelli hosted the first exhibit of Rauschenberg's work in March 1958. Featured in the show were Rauschenberg's combines, including *Bed*, *Rebus*, and

Hymnal. The Hansa Gallery showed several works by its co-founder, Allan Kaprow, as well as an exhibition of life-size plaster sculptures by George Segal.

Downtown, Greenwich Village was further establishing itself as a hotbed of modern art with the opening of the Judson Studio (later Judson Gallery) in the basement of Judson Memorial Church near New York University. The gallery made studio space available to local artists free of charge; among those who took advantage of the church's generosity to show their work in the 1960s were Rauschenberg, Oldenburg, Dine, Wesselman, Red Grooms, and Kaprow, who staged one of the earliest Happenings ("Apple Shrine") there in 1960. Judson Gallery became a cultural, social, and political focal point in that questioning decade, standing as a symbol of both avant-garde art—from painting to poetry to dance—and political activism, as well as an incubator of the civil rights movement, women's movement, and anti–Vietnam War movement.

By the late spring of 1959, Roy Lichtenstein was ready to introduce the world to his newest style. A solo exhibition of his untitled abstract paintings was held at the Condon Riley Gallery (24 E. 67th Street). Most of the works were characterized by scant traces of bright colors played across stark white backgrounds. Like Johns's paintings, some of these used a technique of heavy impasto on the canvas. Unlike Johns's work, however, they did not include any recognizable figurative subject matter. The reception to the show was fairly unenthusiastic. Abstract Expressionism, it seemed, was simply not Lichtenstein's strength. New York's art patrons were ready for something new and

Leo Castelli:
Pioneering Patron of Pop

No single gallery owner had more impact on the 1960s Pop Art explosion—and on Roy Lichtenstein's career—than Leo Castelli. Born in 1907 in Trieste, then in the Austro-Hungarian empire, now a part of Italy, Castelli attended law school in Milan and entered the insurance business before jumping into the art world in the 1930s. Part of the catalyst for the career change was his first wife, Ileana Schapira, the daughter of one of Romania's richest men, whom Castelli met in his firm's Bucharest office. (Ileana became better known to many art lovers as Ileana Sonnabend, an important proponent of American modern art in her own right.)

In 1935 the couple moved to Paris, where they opened their first gallery. Not long afterward, World War II broke out and the Castellis fled Paris for New York City. Leo joined the US Army, serving as an intelligence operative for the Office of Strategic Services (OSS, the predecessor of the modern CIA), and was granted US citizenship after the war in return for his service.

Castelli was always more interested in discovering new artists than in working with known ones, so he did not open a gallery until he found art that he described as having "pure enthusiasm." He found it in Rauschenberg, and then Johns, in 1954. He opened his first New York gallery in midtown in 1957, and he moved to SoHo in 1971, spearheading that area's growth as New York's center of cutting-edge art and culture. Wherever Castelli went, it seemed, New York's art lovers would follow, and as time went on, they often found Roy Lichtenstein's latest on the gallery walls. The careers of the gallery owner and the Pop Artist were inextricably linked throughout four decades, in a tandem that defined New York art for a generation. Castelli and Ileana divorced in 1959, and Castelli remarried twice after that, first to Antoinette Fraissex du Bost (cofounder of Castelli Graphics), who died in 1987, and then to a young Italian art critic, Barbara Bertozzi, who joined him in opening yet another gallery.

Dismissive of the opinions of critics, Castelli always followed his instincts, and his place in the pantheon of American art's major twentieth-century figures indicates that those instincts served him well. Were it not for Castelli's unerring eye for art, Roy Lichtenstein might have been consigned to relative obscurity— teaching art during the day and drawing comic strip confections for his children in his spare time.

radical, even if they were not yet sure exactly what that something would be.

Perhaps on some level, Lichtenstein realized this. At home, he was experimenting with very different types of art, ones that his admirers today might consider far more significant than the Expressionist, nonrepresentational pieces hanging on the walls at the Condon Riley Gallery. He was creating ink drawings of Mickey Mouse, Donald Duck, Bugs Bunny, and other popular cartoon and comic strip characters, partly to entertain his young children. Executed in a loose, improvisational style that owes some-

Allan Kaprow and the First Happenings

Lawrence Alloway and the Independent Group in London may have been the progenitors of Pop, but it was not only the visual arts that were instrumental in its birth. Some of the seeds were also planted by the pioneers of what is now called "performance art."

Allan Kaprow was born in Atlantic City, New Jersey, in 1927. A student of Hans Hoffman's painting school in the 1940s, Kaprow cofounded the Hansa Gallery—a cooperative artists' gallery on East 10th Street in Greenwich Village—in 1952. His early work as a painter displayed the intense action painting motif of Pollock and the Abstract Expressionists, but by the later 1950s, he was following his own dream of breaking out of the box, progressing beyond what he saw as the boundaries of traditional painting, and creating all-enveloping environments—works that would negate the idea of a casual spectator and demand audience participation.

One of his major influences was Pollock, whose work Kaprow examined in a 1958 *ARTNews* article, "The Legacy of Jackson Pollock." Pollock's paintings, Kaprow wrote, "ceased to become paintings and became environments." He believed that such huge, all-embracing paintings could usher in the next creative step, the one where the "action" aspect could overtake the "painting" and become a true interactive experience—what he would later famously call a "Happening."

Another influence on Kaprow was John Cage, the composer of experimental music. In his unique compositions, referred to as "chance music," the elements of the music are left to chance, the movements determined by random fate. Cage was especially notorious for his 4'33" composition, which was a piano piece in which no musical notes were played—an unprecedented experiment supposedly influenced by the white canvases of Robert Rauschenberg, a colleague of Cage's at Black Mountain College.

Kaprow studied with the avant-garde composer when he came to the New School for Social Research in Manhattan between 1956 and 1958. Cage believed that no type of experimentation was too radical or too unorthodox to explore in his own work, and his modernist musical pieces demanded total audience immersion and participation. Cage guided Kaprow to theatrical pieces, which he believed held the greatest potential for the integration of real life and art.

Although other Pop Artists—Rauschenberg, Oldenburg, and Dine among them—had experimented with theatrical pieces, they quickly abandoned them for more traditional areas. Kaprow, in contrast, moved from action paintings to three-dimensional assemblages and collages to the audience-interactive pieces that became a popular and viable art form in the anti-establishment counterculture of the 1960s.

The first event to be called a Happening took place in October 1959 at Manhattan's Reuben Gallery (61 4th Avenue between 9th and 10th). Titled "18 Happenings in 6 Parts," it was a performance the likes of which none of the patrons had ever seen. Visitors to the gallery were given tickets that directed them to specific seats in a series of rooms, where they witnessed such bizarre tableaux as a girl squeezing oranges, an artist lighting matches while painting, and an orchestra playing toy instruments. Jasper Johns and Robert Rauschenberg were involved in the program, each having painted one side of a piece of fabric used in the performance, and also performing. Although the progression of events was scripted, the event had none of the traditional trappings of live theater, such as plot, dialogue, or even professional performers, lending it an air of unstructured spontaneity. By most accounts, the first Happening was a success, and it was even given a favorable review by drama critic Richard Scechner of the *New York Times*.

By 1960, New York's fashionable people were seeking out this trendy new style of performance art, which was rather difficult to find because it was being acted out most often in empty lots, lofts, train stations, and other places off the beaten path for the typical theater patron or museum visitor. Subsequent Happenings pushed the envelope even further than the first one at Reuben Gallery. One called "Coca Cola, Shirley Cannonball?" featured a huge cardboard boot kicking a ball around a gymnasium to the beat of a fife and drum. In another, "A Spring Happening," patrons went into a dark tunnel where they were bombarded with the sound of a power mower and air generated by an electric fan. As a tribute to his painting teacher staged for for the Museum of Modern Art, Kaprow created "Push and Pull: A Furniture Comedy for Hans Hofmann," which was essentially a suite of two rooms with furniture that visitors to the exhibit were encouraged to rearrange.

thing to de Kooning—and not approaching the clean, graphic look of his later comic strip paintings—these small pieces anticipate the stylistic breakthrough that was on the horizon with the dawn of the 1960s.

As the 1960s began, New York City was the place to be for young American artists due to the unprecedented support they were receiving from the new generation of visionary gallery owners. In addition to the Castelli Gallery, which remained on the cutting edge of new trends, the Martha Jackson Gallery (32 E. 69th Street) hosted a handful of shows in 1960 that straddled the stylistic line between the "neo-Dada" movement and what would become known as Pop Art.

January 1960 opened with a show featuring the works of avant-garde "junk sculptor" John Chamberlain, whose stock-in-trade was pieces made from mangled scrap autobody parts. In June, the gallery presented "New Media—New Forms: In Painting and Sculpture," featuring work by Jean Arp, Alexander Calder, Robert Indiana, Johns, Dine, Kaprow, Oldenburg, and a host of others. A second show in October of that year, "New Media—New Forms: In Painting and Sculpture II," continued the increasingly trendy themes of the first, and featured many of the same artists, plus works by Rauschenberg and Lucas Samaras.

JOLTED IN NEW JERSEY

By the spring of 1960, Lichtenstein was again packing to leave the state of New York, though this time he would not go nearly as far, and the move would bring him and his family closer to, not farther from, the New York City art world. He resigned his position at SUNY Oswego to accept a job as assistant professor of art at Douglass College of Rutgers University in New Brunswick, New Jersey. He moved both his residence and his studio to Highland Park, New Jersey.

Lichtenstein had reached his late thirties without finding an artistic voice that was uniquely his own. After years spent painting in the genres and styles of those artists he admired, he opened up to other forms of artistic expression in the late 1950s and 1960s. At Rutgers, he would make the acquaintance of several of the people who were becoming the toast of Manhattan's art-gallery cognoscenti, most notably fellow Rutgers instructor Allan Kaprow. In Lichtenstein's student days, Reginald Marsh's figure drawing classes helped solidify his draftsmanship, and Hoyt Sherman's "flash room" experiments expanded his interest in forms and design. Now an instructor and a working artist, Lichtenstein would receive from his colleague Kaprow the final piece of the puzzle in developing his own mature style.

Lichtenstein attended his first Happening—an informal one at Rutgers—in 1960, and although he was a spectator rather than a participant, it would remain in the back of his mind as he moved closer to his signature style. If a cardboard boot kicking a ball around a gym is as legitimate

The Martha Jackson Gallery

Martha Jackson, née Martha Kellogg, a scion of the family that owned the Kellogg Chemical Company, established the Martha Jackson Gallery in 1953. After marrying in the 1930s, she began volunteering at art museums and attending art history classes at Johns Hopkins University. She began collecting art in 1943, using income from her substantial family trust; her first acquisition was a piece by Marc Chagall. She befriended a number of artists in the 1940s and 1950s, including Pollock, Franz Kline, John Marin, and Lichtenstein's drawing teacher, Reginald Marsh.

The gallery's first show was the well-received, comprehensive exhibit *100 Years of Watercolors,* but Jackson was interested in showing more daring material and nurturing emerging talent. Her gallery became known for exhibiting new art from the United States and Europe in almost any discipline. She was one of the early proponents of Abstract Expressionism (she purchased de Kooning's *Woman* series), though she didn't blindly subscribe to its antifigurative notions; she often displayed figurative art alongside abstract pieces. She showed female artists such as Louise Nevelson, Barbara Hepworth, and Grace Hartigan during a time when women in art had difficulty finding representation. When Pop hit the scene, Jackson's gallery was the first to show Dine, Oldenburg, and Indiana. Her influence on the modern art scene was inestimable: most movements of the late twentieth century got their start at her gallery. Martha Jackson died in 1969. Today, this Upper East Side address still houses art galleries, such as Richard L. Feigen & Company and Hauser and Wirth.

as a performance of *Hamlet*, he may have thought, then why can't a reproduction of a panel from a romance comic be as legitimate as a Picasso abstraction?

In addition to expanding Lichtenstein's mind with Happenings, Kaprow provided the bridge between Lichtenstein and the artists who would be his contemporaries throughout the Pop-dominated early 1960s, introducing him to people such as Claes Oldenburg. Oldenburg was born in Stockholm in 1929, the son of a Swedish consul general. Like Lichtenstein, his earliest painting influences were the Abstract Expressionists. But after moving to New York, meeting Kaprow in 1958, and taking part in Happenings, Oldenburg's art took a radical turn to the neo-Dada plaster-and-garbage constructions and food-replica sculptures for which he has become much better known.

Kaprow also introduced Lichtenstein to Lucas Samaras, a native of Greece who became a US citizen in 1955. Samaras's diverse portfolio included sculptures of rags and plaster and nails and pins, but his real fame did not come until the 1970s, when he released *Autopolaroids*—a series of close-up photos of his own anatomy. Through Kaprow, Lichtenstein also became acquainted with George Segal, a New Yorker who became known for using plaster-soaked gauze medical bandages to cast scenes of anonymous people in everyday life. All these artists reflected the influence of Kaprow in their work, and it was inevitable that contact with these future contemporaries would set Lichtenstein on a similar path away from the mainstream.

Lichtenstein was still primarily a teacher in 1960. In addition to his duties at Douglass, he began teaching adult classes in painting and drawing at the photography and art center at Princeton University in September. All the while, he was also painting and exhibiting. Although he was being introduced to lots of new ideas, Lichtenstein's works for public consumption at this time were still mostly nonrepresentational abstractions.

At an exhibit at Douglass in January 1961, Lichtenstein showed twelve abstract pictures done by applying ribbons of paint with torn-up bedsheets (one picture used pieces of nailed-together refrigerator-crate plywood as a canvas). He was still determined to get his untitled abstract pieces into the galleries in New York, and the gallery that had become the holy grail to young artists in the city was Leo Castelli's. In the fall of 1961, Lichtenstein finally had the opportunity to meet Castelli and his wife, Ileana, and to show the gallery owner his abstract canvases. Castelli did not immediately agree to represent the eager Lichtenstein, but the two men struck up a relationship that would prove to be highly profitable to them both in the coming years.

BUBBLEGUM ART

Although Lichtenstein and Andy Warhol had not yet met, or even heard of each other, both were experimenting with images from the comics. Warhol produced paintings with images from *Popeye*, *Nancy*, and *Dick Tracy* comic strips, done in the loose-brushstroke style of Abstract Expressionism. In April 1961, New Yorkers got their first taste of

Les Nouveaux Réalistes

A milestone show in Europe in April 1960 showcased another group of artists who would be linked to American Pop. "Les Nouveaux Réalistes" (the New Realists) were officially formed at the home of Yves Klein in Paris in October 1960. The group included Arman, Jean Tinguely, Raymond Hains, César, Martial Raysse, Mimmo Rotella, Niki de Saint Phalle, Daniel Spoerri, Klein himself, and the artist known as Christo, whose actual last name is Javacheff. Several of these artists had exhibited their works at the Galleria Apollinaire in Milan in April. That show's catalog featured the publication of the trailblazing New Realist manifesto by art scholar Pierre Restany, a treatise on the changing nature of art that would help pave the way for Pop and other movements of the late twentieth century.

The manifesto pointed out the tendency of all forms of art to "ossify," or exhaust themselves, and stressed the necessity of art to identify with the modern world, or what Restany considered the "real" and "sublime."

"What is being proposed?" Restany asked hypothetically:

> The exciting adventure of the real seen for what it is and not through the prism of conceptual or imaginative transmission. . . . Sociology comes to the aid of consciousness and hazard, whether it is in the posting or the tearing down of a sign, the physical appearance of an object, the rubbish from a house or livingroom, the unleashing of mechanical affectivity, or the expanding of sensitivity beyond the limits of its perception. . . . People, if they succeed in reintegrating themselves

with what is real, will identify it with their own transcendence, which is emotion, feeling, and, ultimately, poetry.

The sentiment was one that Allan Kaprow could appreciate—and one that the proponents of Abstract Expressionism would have regarded as heresy. In the United States, a whole generation of artists was eager to associate themselves with the "real," even though, in Lichtenstein's case, he hadn't quite acquainted himself with how to do so.

But the old generation wasn't ready to fade away just yet. Willem de Kooning, in particular, had disdain for this new style of art and an increasing antipathy toward the gallery owners who promoted it. An example that illustrates the rift involves de Kooning's criticism of Leo Castelli. Irked at Castelli's interest in the new art and his ability to sell it to collectors, de Kooning said, "That son of a bitch Castelli, give him a couple of beer cans and he'll sell them." Johns, upon hearing of these comments, promptly created another of his famous proto-Pop works—a trompe l'oeil sculpture of two bronze cylinders painted to resemble Ballantine Ale beer cans. Castelli, naturally, displayed the piece and sold it. The winds of artistic taste were clearly shifting.

Warhol's advertising and comic strip images, displayed behind the mannequins in the windows of Bonwit Teller.

In Highland Park around the same time, Roy Lichtenstein was presented with what would prove to be the most significant challenge of his life as an artist—one posed by his own children. Lichtenstein had been inserting cartoon images into his semiabstract works but had never created a full-fledged cartoon image, and this, apparently, was what his children wanted to see. Art world legend has it that one of Lichtenstein's sons pointed at a bubblegum wrapper showing a couple of popular cartoon characters and began ribbing his father, saying something to the effect of "Daddy, I'll bet you can't paint pictures as good as this." Lichtenstein's response to this good-natured prodding (if it ever really happened; in his typically enigmatic fashion, Lichtenstein never confirmed or denied this account, and no researcher has found evidence of an actual gum wrapper that depicted the characters he used) was both a turning point in his career and a benchmark of the Pop Art movement. (In a synopsis of *Look, Mickey* on its website, the National Gallery of Art identifies the source of the work as a 1960 Disney children's book called *Donald Duck: Lost and Found*, making it even more likely that the bubblegum wrapper story is apocryphal.)

In early 1961, Lichtenstein showed Kaprow his semiabstract paintings with cartoon characters and continued to experiment with the subject. *Look, Mickey*, painted in the summer of 1961, was a major stylistic departure for Lichtenstein: the image is a seemingly whimsical and innocent one centered around two iconic Walt Disney characters, in which the expressionistic brushstrokes of his past three years' work were nowhere to be found, supplanted by hard edges (even visible pencil marks) and a crude version of his now-trademark Ben-Day dots that approximated the four-color printing process in extreme close-up. The painting is also Lichtenstein's first use of another of his signature devices, the comic book dialogue balloon. The Ben-Day dot technique was applied with a plastic-bristle dog-grooming brush dipped in oil paint—the most painterly way that Lichtenstein would ever apply this technique, which would become increasingly (and intentionally) mechanized and impersonal in his future paintings.

The ironic humor in *Look, Mickey* is obvious, though art historians and critics have long speculated about a deeper meaning in the historic painting, the first in which Lichtenstein directly appropriated imagery from a panel of comic art. In his book *Image Duplicator*, critic Michael Lobel posits that the placement of the figures—Donald, ignorant of his humiliating situation, near the bottom of the composition, and Mickey, smug in his knowledge of Donald's plight, near the top—represented the relationship between high and low culture, a gulf that Pop Art was destined to bridge. "The painting," he says, "presents a scene in which a seemingly momentous discovery comes at the price of an equally profound degradation."

Whether or not any message about art, culture, or society was intended in *Look, Mickey*, most critics agree that it was the subject matter itself that announced the arrival of its creator with a bang. In a discussion of Lichtenstein's life and work following the artist's death, *Washington Post* art critic Paul Richard told an interviewer:

> Well, if you can imagine how "shocking" it was to see a comic strip on the wall of Leo Castelli's gallery in 1962, it got a lot of attention. . . . Previously there had been things on the wall that were just blank canvases or active

brushstrokes. And suddenly he took what was kind of an illegitimate subject for art and painted it in such a way that when you saw the object . . . on the wall, it said, "I am a serious painting." And people believed it.

For Lichtenstein, *Look, Mickey* was simply a logical extension of the subject matter that was being explored by Kaprow in his Happenings and by Jasper Johns in his object paintings. The idea that one panel of a comic strip, isolated and enlarged to massive proportions, could serve as an individual piece of art was a radical concept—one that would engage Lichtenstein for the better part of the next decade, perplex art critics, confound proponents of the source material, and eventually find a widespread affirmation by a generation of art collectors.

Look, Mickey would not be seen by the public until the following year. But with his newfound interest in reproducing printed matter on a large scale, Lichtenstein had hit upon a style. That same summer (1961), he created his first paintings based on consumer advertisement images, including *Keds*, *Washing Machine*, and *Girl with Ball* (taken from a newspaper ad for Mount Airy Lodge, a resort in New York's Pocono region).

Like Warhol (who would become associated with such consumer subject matter, as Lichtenstein would with comic and cartoon imagery), Lichtenstein had developed a fascination with the "low art" of the consumer culture that had largely taken over the United States in the decade following World War II, and his experience as a commercial artist and draftsman gave him an affinity for it that few at the time could equal.

Another aspect of advertising art of the day was the "before and after" scenes that showed the usefulness of a product. These led to Lichtenstein's diptych works, such as *Bread in Bag* and *Step-on Can with Leg* (which depicts the leg of an early 1960s housewife demonstrating the use of a trash can with a pedal-operated lid, a new and innovative kitchen appliance at the time). By the time he was working on these paintings, he had invented other methods of applying his ersatz printer dots that further removed the artist's hands from the process, such as using a paint roller over a handmade metal screen to distribute the paint over the canvas, and then using a small scrub brush to push paint through.

a CRUCIaL Connection

By the fall of 1961, Allan Kaprow was impressed enough with what he'd seen from Lichtenstein that he arranged an introduction to Ivan Karp, the director of the Leo Castelli Gallery. Karp and Lichtenstein, it turned out, had a few things in common. Both were native New Yorkers (Karp was born in the Bronx, and grew up in Brooklyn and Queens); both had an aptitude for art from a very early age (Karp spent many weekends of his childhood visiting the Brooklyn Museum and getting to know the work of the artists displayed there); and both had served a stint in the US military (Karp was trained as a gunnery mechanic in the Army Air Forces). After dabbling in filmmaking and writing art criticism (notably for early issues of the *Village Voice*), Karp bounced around to several New York galleries in the 1950s, including Hansa and Martha Jackson, and came to work for Castelli in 1959.

Karp was the primary "talent scout" for Castelli, with an eye for what was fresh and exciting. The day Lichtenstein walked into the gallery was an important day for Pop Art as a movement of like-minded creators. Not only was it the day Lichtenstein got his first glimpse of the work of Warhol and James Rosenquist, it was also the turning point for his own career. Perhaps finally acknowledging that Abstract Expressionism (or perhaps just his own attempts at it) was not what Castelli was looking for, Lichtenstein brought a handful of his 1961 works—*Look, Mickey*, *The Refrigerator*, *Girl with Ball*, and *Step-on Can with Leg*—to the gallery.

In an interview in 1969 for the Smithsonian Institution's Archives of American Art, Karp related the story of that fateful meeting:

> Allan Kaprow . . . called me on the phone one afternoon and said there was a painter and teacher working out at Douglass College . . . who was doing some rather unsettling images. And Kaprow asked me if I would be so kind as to look at them. I said, "Yes, it's all right to bring them to the gallery." Apparently the artist brought them in on top of his car from Rutgers one afternoon when he wasn't teaching. I remember seeing Roy in the hall with them. They were all facing the wall. I said, "What are these?" He said, "Well, Mr. Kaprow called about me. I'm Lichtenstein and I wish you'd look at these paintings." He turned them around . . . and it was a very jarring experience. I remember the first thing I said to him: "You really can't do this, you know."

> It was just too shocking for words that somebody
> should celebrate the cartoon and the commercial image
> like that. And they were cold and blank and bold and over-
> whelming. I remember saying to myself, He can't do this,
> he just can't do this. I said it to him aloud. He said, "Well,
> I seem to be caught up in it. Here they are."

Leaving out *Look, Mickey* (which Karp unapologetically
disliked, referring to it as "a little mushy cartoon picture"),
Karp sent the work on to Castelli—who had a similar set of
conflicting reactions, though he took a particular interest
in *Girl with Ball*. Ultimately, several weeks after his momentous visit, Lichtenstein got what he wanted: the representation of the hottest modern art gallery in New York.

Lichtenstein's meeting with Karp in 1961 was also significant for the effect it had on Andy Warhol's art. Warhol
was at that time searching for a truly individual style and
experimenting with many devices similar to the ones Lichtenstein was developing, notably advertisements, product
imagery, and comics. Warhol visited the Castelli Gallery
shortly after Lichtenstein did and glimpsed *Girl with Ball*.
Lichtenstein, in turn, visited Warhol's Manhattan studio
(1342 Lexington Avenue) with Karp, and saw Warhol's
comic strip paintings, along with his works based on consumer goods. It is certainly not a coincidence that shortly
afterward, one artist veered in one direction and the other,
in another. Like many New York artists at the time, Warhol
craved representation by Leo Castelli, and he reasoned that
since Lichtenstein already had the comic strips covered as
a specialty, his best bet was not to be seen as imitating or
competing with those works. In his 1969 interview, Karp
recalled the experience firsthand:

I didn't know who Warhol was or what he did. All I knew was that he was a man with a crop of gray hair who came in and bought a Jasper Johns [drawing] from me. He issued one of his curious little sounds like an astonished "Oh!" that he says every so often. . . . He said, "Good God"—or whatever he was exclaiming—"I'm doing something like this myself!!". . . He was really shocked and at the same time he was appalled. And I think he was very concerned that somebody else was doing the same thing. . . . I saw the paintings [at Warhol's studio] and they were, as he said, cartoon subjects. Some of them were very lyrical, unlike Roy's paintings, which were pretty stark and straightforward and cold to begin with. Andy still had the echo of abstract expressionism in his brushwork and things. We were just beginning to launch Lichtenstein . . . it would be a very destructive thing to have these two new artists doing the same sort of thing.

Obviously, Warhol not only convinced Castelli to represent him (though not until 1963), but he found a great deal of success with his own distinctive style in the 1960s. Today, it's interesting to speculate what place Roy Lichtenstein might have had in the Pop Art pantheon if Warhol had gotten to Castelli first.

5

SEE YOU IN THE FUNNY PAGES

COMICS CONQUER THE GALLERIES

By October 1961, Lichtenstein's first works had been consigned to Leo Castelli Gallery, and he was receiving a $400 monthly stipend from it. It did not take long for *Girl with Ball*—the painting that had initially caught the eye of the savvy Castelli—to sell, to architect Philip Johnson. Other sales followed as the year came to a close.

Spending more and more time at the gallery, Lichtenstein met two of his contemporaries, already regarded as giants—Jasper Johns and Robert Rauschenberg. By most accounts, the Pop artists of the 1960s—including Johns and Rauschenberg, who were the movement's forefathers—were mostly friendly with each other despite their professional rivalry, perhaps united in a common front against the Abstract Expressionists, who would just as soon have seen all these irreverent young upstarts disappear.

SINGLE IN THE CITY

If Lichtenstein's professional life was hitting new heights in 1961, his personal life was going in the opposite direction. By the autumn, his marriage to Isabel, perhaps straining under the demands of Roy's revitalized artistic career—as well as Isabel's reported alcoholism—had become troubled, and the couple agreed to a trial separation. Although the circumstances necessitating the move were far from ideal, Lichtenstein returned to New York City, settling for a brief time into a residence and studio on Broad Street in what is today the city's downtown financial district.

As Lichtenstein rang in the new year as a slightly richer, slightly more well known, newly separated bachelor artist in Manhattan, another recently opened gallery was making its own contribution to the gathering momentum of the Pop movement. The Green Gallery (15 W. 57th Street), opened by Richard Bellamy in the fall of 1960, sponsored Claes Oldenburg in his major contribution to Pop Art's heyday, *Ray Gun Manufacturing Co.*, in a former furniture warehouse in New York's Alphabet City (107 E. 2nd Street).

The Green Gallery would ultimately host Lichtenstein's work as well, and Bellamy himself would become a subject of a Lichtenstein painting—albeit in a decidedly oblique way. *Mr. Bellamy* (1961) is one of the few notable examples of Lichtenstein's early 1960s work that seems to be cheekily self-referential. In it, a handsome, square-jawed airplane pilot strides toward a meeting with a superior below a comic book thought balloon that says, "I am supposed to report to a Mr. Bellamy. I wonder what he's like." The scene may indicate the beginning of a high-flying adventure story, with the hero getting his mission details. But most likely, the pilot is a stand-in for the artist, his thoughts referring to Lichtenstein's nervousness in meeting the gallery owner. *Mr. Bellamy* was also one of the first Lichtenstein paintings that more closely approximated the four-color printing process, with dots of different sizes and color densities conveying tonal variations in the areas of color. The work of Milt Caniff, of *Steve Roper* and *Terry and the Pirates* fame, has been cited as possible source material for the pilot in *Mr. Bellamy*, although it is unclear whether Lichtenstein appropriated any specific image.

Lichtenstein's sense of humor was on display in a pair of portraits, exhibited at Castelli's in 1962, that were a tribute of a sort to the two men who were instrumental in his revitalized career. *Portrait of Ivan Karp* and *Portrait of Allan Kaprow* not only were done in Lichtenstein's emerging cartoon style, they were basically the same picture, and neither subject looks much like Karp or Kaprow. Each painting displays a clean-cut, clean-shaven stereotype of a 1950s-era young man. By using a generic, inexpressive face to characterize two very different men in the art world, Lichtenstein may have been making his own bold statement about the depersonalization of the new art. If so, there is no evidence in the body of Lichtenstein's 1960s work that he felt this was a bad thing. Quite the contrary: becoming more like a machine, removing the artist's physical presence from the canvas, became a theme that he explored in one way or another for the rest of his life.

If the general public was becoming aware of a new style of art in 1961, this style was nearly impossible to avoid by 1962. The art cognoscenti were the first to sense the coming wave, but by the end of the year, anyone picking up a copy of *Newsweek*, *Life*, or *Good Housekeeping* was likely to be exposed to it in one way or another. Pop Art—though it had yet to be dubbed officially or even recognized as a movement when the year dawned—was truly "popular" art, engaging the masses at the same time that it undoubtedly confused many of them. Many armchair critics in the 1950s looked at the Abstract Expressionism of a Pollock or a de Kooning and groused, "My kid could do that!" or "This is art?" Pop engendered many of the same responses (even among the well-educated art critics), but somehow it was different. If people disliked an Abstract Expressionist piece, it was because they saw a mass of nonrepresentational strokes of color that they could not relate to or understand. If people disliked a Pop Art piece, it was because they recognized what it was, and decided for themselves that this was not, in fact, art. However, in New York City— the beating heart of the controversial movement, where a sense of sophistication, an open-mindedness, and a desire to be on the cultural cutting edge of the nation were taking hold in the postwar generation—Pop was the next big thing. And Lichtenstein was on the verge of becoming a household name in his beloved hometown.

BLASTING INTO THE BIG TIME

Roy Lichtenstein's arrival into the proverbial big time occurred, appropriately enough, at the Leo Castelli Gallery, which held its first solo exhibition of his work from February 10 to March 3, 1962. By the time the show opened, the artist had done his first work in the two genres for which he became well known: romance comics and war comics.

Although some critics have tried to attach political or social significance to the works done with these themes—pointing out the anti–Vietnam War sentiment among the youth of the 1960s and the decade's transformation of traditional female roles—Lichtenstein's statement probably had more to do with mass-consumer depictions of masculinity and femininity than with anything else. "His comic strip images of the 1960s explored the stock signifiers of American mass culture," David Hopkins states in *After Modern Art: 1945–2000*. "Square jaws connoted maleness, blonde hair and tears femininity. Gender roles were further demarcated into spheres of combat (Lichtenstein's men are often at war in unspecified Asian locations, hinting at American involvement in Vietnam) and the domestic bedroom (women invariably agonize over love affairs)."

The Refrigerator and *Engagement Ring*, both displayed in the 1962 show, are two examples of Lichtenstein's woman-centered work. *The Refrigerator* depicts a close-up of a smiling suburban housewife wiping out the tray of a refrigerator, an image that could have been—and probably was—taken straight from a print advertisement for some cleaning agent or another. In *Engagement Ring*, a concerned-looking blonde woman strokes her chin as a male companion looks on in the background. "It's . . . it's not an engagement ring, is it?" reads the woman's dialogue balloon, leaving the viewer to wonder about the context of the scene—what was said before it, what was said after.

The effects of pulling a panel out of an imagined sequence (in the case of *Engagement Ring*, the original was a frame from the *Winnie Winkle* comic strip, by Martin Branner, published in the July 16, 1961, edition of the *Chicago Tribune*), letting it speak for itself, letting the tension of "What's next?" linger in the viewer's mind—all these are part of the charm of Lichtenstein's comic book images. It was in these early works that Lichtenstein established the prototypical Lichtenstein woman—usually blonde, usually emotional, and so stereotypically perfect in form, face, and figure that she was somehow unreal. Much has been written about Lichtenstein's women and what statement they were making. The artist himself stayed characteristically vague on the subject throughout his life, but students of his work have ventured some opinions. "None of the beauty that appears in his work is real," said Elizabeth Richardson in a 1993 profile in *Harper's Bazaar*.

It is an evocation of an entirely fictional femininity, drawn secondhand from a presentation of beauty so common and codified that it's lifeless and cold. . . . *Girl with Ball* [1961] is not a picture of a girl at all. It's a painting of a picture of a girl, copied from an advertisement . . . while the sunbather with the beach ball who inhabits it is not entirely incidental, neither is she an organic expression of

Lichtenstein's attitude toward her—for she does not, of course, exist.

Blam was one of the earliest examples of Lichtenstein's many war-themed canvases. Depicting a fighter pilot ejecting from his exploding aircraft, with huge, bright bursts of red-and-orange flames, this painting traces its origin to a panel in issue #89 of *All-American Men of War* by artist Russ Heath, published by DC Comics in January and February 1962. The huge sound effect for which the painting is named (*Whaam!*, 1963, and *Takka Takka*, 1962, are other famous examples) was another comic book staple that had never before been seen in gallery art. It was as if Lichtenstein were exploring the two extremes of male and female stereotypes: men were involved in violence and war, while women were caught up in emotional hysteria. The statement, whether intended or not, had a peculiar resonance in the 1960s, an era during which traditional gender roles were questioned and challenged like never before.

In later years, Heath—who provided the comic book source material for *Whaam!* as well as for *Blam*—would express dissatisfaction with Lichtenstein profiting so handsomely from those works. In 2014, at age eighty-four, Heath wrote and drew an original comic strip for the Hero Initiative, a nonprofit organization set up to help comic book creators in financial need, in which he lamented that *Whaam!* earned "four million" for Lichtenstein while Heath "got zero." In his scathing introduction to the strip on the Comics Alliance website, Chris Sims writes:

With six decades of work under his belt, Russ Heath is arguably one of the most important creators in comics. It was his art that was, to put it charitably, "adapted" by Roy Lichtenstein for the pop art pieces that made him famous. Of course, as is unfortunately so often the case for hard-working creators in comics, while Lichtenstein made millions lightboxing panels Heath had drawn in the pages of DC's romance and war comics, Heath himself never saw a dime, despite continuing a career that saw him become one of the most respected elder statesmen of the industry.

Nevertheless, the solo Lichtenstein show at the Castelli Gallery was a watermark for this new and intriguing art movement. *Newsweek* reviewed the show, as did *Arts* magazine's Donald Judd. By June 1962, Castelli had included Lichtenstein's pen-and-ink drawings—showing them publicly for the first time—in the group exhibition *Drawings: Lee Bontecou, Jasper Johns, Roy Lichtenstein, Robert Moskowitz, Robert Rauschenberg, Jack Tworkov*. *Life* magazine ran an article in its June 15 issue on what it referred to as the new art, with Lichtenstein as one of the featured artists.

Lichtenstein, Warhol, Rosenquist, Oldenburg, and Dine were all coming into their own in 1962, and many of them were by now acquainted, but it was an article in the March issue of *Art International* that linked them for the first time under the banner of a new artistic movement. "'Pop' Culture, Metaphysical Disgust, and the New Vulgarians," by art commentator Max Kozloff, took a negative look at his subjects, opining that "with Oldenburg, Lichtenstein, and Rosenquist, not to speak of Robert Indiana, the spectator's nose is practically rubbed into the whole pointless cajolery of our hardshell, sign-dominated culture."

Although Kozloff was hardly alone in his assessment of the attributes (or lack thereof) of this new commercial style of art, his "New Vulgarians" label would fortunately not stick. Critic Gene R. Swenson of *ARTNews* came up with a slightly less pejorative epithet, the "New American Sign Painters," in his September 1962 article. The first name that came to be applied to Lichtenstein and company was actually one cribbed from their European predecessors— the "New Realists." That sobriquet was used in another landmark show in 1962, the *International Exhibition of the New Realists*, hosted by the Sidney Janis Gallery (15 E. 57th Street) from October 31 to December 1. The roster of artists included several of the original "Nouveaux Réalistes" from the *Galleria Apollinaire* show in Milan in 1960, Klein and Tinguely among them, as well as Dine, Rosenquist, Segal, Warhol, and Lichtenstein. The gallery was founded in 1948 by Sidney Janis from Buffalo, New York, who in his younger years made a name in vaudeville as a ballroom dancer. As an adult, he started a successful shirt-making company, and he and his wife, Harriet, developed a passion for collecting art. On their frequent trips to Paris, they met Picasso, Mondrian, Brancusi, Léger, and other contemporary artists. By the time they moved to New York City in the 1930s, the couple had amassed a respectable collection, and Sidney joined the advisory board of the Museum of Modern Art, eventually closing his shirt-making business in 1939 to devote himself full time to writing about art.

Sidney Janis was fifty-two when he opened the gallery, which quickly became known for exhibiting works by Mondrian, Léger, the Futurists, and the Fauvists. By the 1950s, it was renowned as an outlet for the American avant-garde, hosting the first of three solo Jackson Pollock shows, and eventually representing Kline, Motherwell, Rothko, Adolph Gottlieb, Joseph Albers, and others. With Sidney Janis's lifelong collector's eye for valuable art, it was only natural that his gallery would showcase the work of Lichtenstein, destined to become one of the most collectible artists in American history.

The *New Realist* exhibition struck some observers and critics as having a common theme: namely, food and that modern-day purveyor of food, the American supermarket, which was becoming commonplace in postwar United States. Lichtenstein's *The Refrigerator* was one of the featured pieces, along with Oldenburg's plaster-of-Paris sculptures of hot dogs and roasts, and Andy Warhol's legendary *200 Campbell's Soup Cans*. The perceived obsession with food earned this group of artists yet another name, bestowed by *Time* magazine in its review: the "Slice of Cake School." Many of the same artists would revisit food subjects in a large way a few years hence at the *American Supermarket* exhibition—a show that would prove to be a significant one for Roy Lichtenstein, who would meet his second wife during preparations for the exhibition.

Only one piece still had to fall into place: officially naming this artistic movement that was taking the culture by storm. "Slice of Cake School" simply wouldn't do. On December 13, 1962, a symposium was held at the Museum of Modern Art, moderated by Peter Selz, the museum's curator of painting and sculpture exhibitions. The audience included a number of notables, among them Lichtenstein, Warhol, Rosenquist, and "the old master" himself, Marcel

Duchamp. "New Realists" was one of the names discussed and eventually rejected. "Neo-Dada" was another, ultimately turned down because the art in question bore only a superficial resemblance to that of the Dada movement, and was not intended as a conscious rebellion against bourgeois conformity, as was Dada. In the end, "Pop Art" won out.

Ironically, Lichtenstein, especially in his later years, would resist being pigeonholed as a Pop artist, because, as he once said, "people use the word 'Pop' to differentiate it from art." But the artistic movement that had started in earnest with his lighthearted picture of Mickey Mouse and Donald Duck now had its name, and he was there for the christening.

Lichtenstein's melodramatic canvases depicting weeping, emotional women became more prevalent in 1963. Asked years later why the women in his art tended to be so wrapped up in overwrought drama, Lichtenstein coyly replied, "Well, I was in the middle of a divorce. I don't know if that had an effect, but it might have."

Indeed, the Lichtensteins' marriage was all but over by 1963, with Isabel moving to Princeton with their two children. The trial separation in late 1961 had been short-lived, as Roy had returned to their Highland Park home in 1962, but ultimately the couple could not make the marriage work. Lichtenstein took a leave of absence from Douglass College and moved his residence and workplace to Manhattan, to what is today regarded as Chelsea (36 W. 26th Street). The loss of his marriage and regular contact with his children surely had an emotional effect, even on someone as work-driven as Lichtenstein apparently was at the time, but relocating to his hometown seemed to energize him creatively.

The artist was producing work at a good clip in 1963, partly because he had taken another step toward depersonalizing the painting process by hiring assistants to apply the Ben-Day dots to his canvases. The handmade metal screen he had previously used was replaced with one that was manufactured, further removing the painter's hand from the painting. The demand for more Lichtenstein, more comic strip mini-dramas, more Pop Art in general, was hitting a fever pitch in 1963, and Lichtenstein—reviled by some critics but the darling of actual art buyers—was quite prepared to meet it.

Thanks to Castelli, the phenomenon was moving beyond New York to the rest of the nation's galleries and museums. Castelli loaned several of Lichtenstein's paintings to the William Rockhill Nelson Gallery of Art and the Atkins Museum of Fine Arts in Kansas City, Missouri, for the *Popular Art: Artistic Projections of Common American Symbols* exhibition in April. Other works were shown at galleries in Washington, DC; Los Angeles; and Houston (the cheekily named *Pop Goes the Easel* exhibition). Perhaps the most significant event for Lichtenstein in 1963 occurred in June, with the first solo exhibition of his work in Europe. The Galerie Ileana Sonnabend in Paris, which hosted the landmark show, was founded by Ileana Sonnabend, the ex-wife of Leo Castelli. Sonnabend became known as the "mom of Pop Art" because of her support for Lichtenstein, Warhol, Dine, Segal, and other members of the movement. She married Michael Sonnabend in 1960, and the couple moved to Europe with the goal of introducing the new American art there. Despite initial resistance, they were largely successful, and while her ex-husband was helping Pop Art conquer New York, Ileana Sonnabend became its ambassador to the rest of the world. Like Castelli, she would be a major factor in making New York's SoHo area the hotbed of Modern art at the beginning of the 1970s.

Lawrence Alloway, the critic who played a significant role in the rise of Pop's European predecessors, turned his eye toward America, which he now recognized as the center of the action in the evolving art scene. He organized a show called *Six Painters and the Object*, which debuted at the Guggenheim Museum on March 14, 1963. Lichtenstein was represented, along with Dine, Johns, Rauschenberg, Rosenquist, and Warhol. The show traveled throughout the United States, spreading the Pop gospel to the heartland.

Comics and Culture

It is impossible to fully understand the appeal of Roy Lichtenstein's early 1960s work without realizing the impact that comic books—and their iconic characters—were having on the culture of the era. The comic book publishing industry was ruled in the 1960s, as it is today, by two giant companies founded in New York City: DC (now headquartered in Burbank, California, and today a division of the Time-Warner multimedia conglomerate) and Marvel (currently located at 135 W. 50th St., and today owned by Disney). DC is the older of the two, founded in 1934 as National Allied Publications, and is the proprietor of Superman, Batman, Wonder Woman, the Flash, and Green Lantern, among many others. The publisher that would become Marvel also started in the 1930s, but traces its modern-day incarnation as a producer of superhero comics back to the landmark first issue of *Fantastic Four* in 1961. In addition to the FF, Marvel counts among its stable of popular characters Spider-Man, the X-Men, the Hulk, and Captain America.

The years after World War II were an era of steady decline for the comics industry, largely due to the 1954 publication of a book called *Seduction of the Innocent* by psychiatrist Fredric Wertham that linked comics with juvenile delinquency. Subsequently, publishers were forced to adhere to a strict code that stifled creativity. But the late 1950s and early 1960s were a fertile period for both major comics companies, owing to the visionary ideas of a new generation of creators. DC innovators such as Julius Schwartz, Gardner Fox, Carmine Infantino, Joe Kubert, Gil Kane, and

Murphy Anderson reimagined the company's World War II—era heroes in a new science fiction—inspired style, while Marvel's Stan Lee, Jack Kirby, and Steve Ditko were imbuing their costumed crime fighters with never-before-seen depth of character, including teenage angst, love triangles, rebellion against authority, and other soap opera trappings, including cliffhangers between issues, tight continuity, and a shared "universe" between the various characters. Comics, which for their first several decades were targeted mainly at young children, were beginning to explore subject matter that could hold the attention of adolescents and young adults, particularly college students.

The success of the superhero titles brought about experimentation with other genres. DC and Marvel added (and in some cases, resurrected) war titles such as *Sgt. Rock, G.I. Combat, All-American Men of War,* and *Sgt. Fury and His Howling Commandos,* and girls' romance series such as *Young Romance, Secret Hearts, Patsy Walker,* and *Millie the Model.* Except in a few notable cases (*Image Duplicator, Mad Scientist*) it was the war and romance books that interested Lichtenstein, and they became his favorite subject matter until he began exploring other topics in late 1964.

Comics, although still considered the lowest form of both art and literature, were becoming part of the fabric of popular culture in the 1960s. To a public accustomed to seeing Batman on television (and to college students writing term papers analyzing Spider-Man's psyche), a massive comic book panel displayed on the walls of an art gallery must have seemed audacious but also acceptable.

Author Les Daniels, writing on the history of DC Comics, postulates that Lichtenstein's use of comic images was more a comment on the relevance of comics as a medium than a celebration of them as an art form. "By putting a frame around comic book images," Daniels writes, "Pop Art simultaneously exalted and debased the medium. It was a way of looking at the work as an artifact of an obsolete culture, as a museum piece. The challenge for DC would be to rise above this left-handed compliment and produce work that readers could continue to recognize as relevant."

Whether or not Lichtenstein intended such a "compliment," a valid argument can be made that the artist's use of comic book imagery in work that proved popular and valuable across the world did more to enhance the relevance of American comic books as an art form than anything before or since. (One might also argue, however, that the proliferation of these characters and their mythologies in popular films and TV series, which began in earnest in the early twenty-first century, has brought them and their source material even more into the mainstream of popular culture.) Marvel, for a time, not only acknowledged Pop's connection to comics, but attempted to cash in on it: their comics' trade dress included a "Pop Art Productions" logo for a short period in the 1960s.

IS THIS ART?

In his Manhattan studio, Lichtenstein was further honing his technique. By the fall of 1963, he had added another mechanical component to his repertoire, an opaque projector that he used to enlarge and project onto a large wall-mounted canvas the tiny originals from the comics pages he was still using as sources. Thus, Lichtenstein could now literally trace the lines of the original onto the canvas with pencil and manipulate them as he saw fit for the design and composition of the finished work. Another evolution in his style was also taking shape concurrently, as visible pencil lines began disappearing from the final work. Lichtenstein was methodically removing as much of the painter's idiom from his pieces as possible, generating finished product that began to bear more and more resemblance to massive four-color prints churned out by a machine.

Even amid the cultural phenomenon that Pop Art was becoming, some—mostly comic book illustrators doing commercial work for hire and often by committee— took issue with Lichtenstein's well-publicized custom of using the work of other artists, deeming it a form of plagiarism. Lichtenstein's *I Can See the Whole Room—and There's Nobody in It!* became a topic of discussion when the May 17, 1963, edition of *Time* magazine printed a letter from cartoonist William Overgard, who claimed that the image on Lichtenstein's canvas was appropriated from the final panel of his *Steve Roper* comic strip published on August 6, 1961. The magazine printed the original panel next to the painting, and the similarities were indeed obvious. But it was the subtle differences that Lichtenstein and his supporters cited—the touches that make a Lichtenstein more than simply a huge "copy" of another work. *Washington Post* art critic Paul Richard discussed the issue in 1997:

If you look at the comics he was "copying" and paintings that resulted when he was through, they really don't look very much alike at all. He would thicken a line . . . or adjust the composition or the sort of abstract qualities. If you don't know that you were looking at a comic strip, you would think this was a very elegant and very cunningly designed piece of work.

Nevertheless, the debate as to the legitimacy of Lichtenstein's comic strip work continues to this day. As recently as 2013, London's Orbital Comics Gallery presented an exhibition in which contemporary comics artists and illustrators "reappropriated" Lichtenstein's paintings as the source material for new original works as a commentary on "the process of appropriation." In an interview with the UK publication *Creative Review*, curator Rian Hughes said:

Almost every painting [Lichtenstein] ever did was appropriated without asking permission or paying royalties. If he was a musician, he would be facing a copyright lawsuit. . . . If you unearthed a rare song and sampled it, people would take great delight in pointing out the source material. Yet in the art world, the source material—particularly when it is created by commercial instead of fine artists—is often treated as if it is some kind of cultural clip art—"low" art that fine artists will elevate to "high" art.

September 28 saw the debut of Lichtenstein's second solo exhibition at the Leo Castelli Gallery, which featured notable works, such as *Drowning Girl*, *Whaam!*, *Torpedo . . . Los!*, and one of Lichtenstein's rare non–comic strip paintings of that year, *Baseball Manager*. Reaction was similar to the response to the first show, with art collectors and gallery patrons impressed and critics' reviews ranging from positive to confused to outraged.

In his review of the show for the *New York Times* (scathingly titled "Lichtenstein: Doubtful but Definite Triumph of the Banal"), Brian O'Doherty devoted a good portion of his commentary to exploring the notion of whether Lichtenstein's art was truly art at all:

> The first argument that fills the vacuum around Mr. Lichtenstein's paintings is whether he reproduces his comic strip originals or whether he transforms them. Lichtenstein experts say his work shows slight differences from the originals, proving that he doesn't transcribe but transforms like a good artist should, differences it takes a Lichtenstein expert to find. . . . It's not a new game. Marcel Duchamp, the old master of innovation, started it all years ago by setting up his ready-mades (suitcases, a urinal, etc.) and calling them art, leaving us the burden of proof they were not.

Although Lichtenstein undoubtedly bristled at the accusation that he was not making art, he probably appreciated the comparison to Duchamp. Whatever the case, 1963 was the year that Lichtenstein created the painting that is widely seen as the response to the criticism of his work and its originality. *Image Duplicator* is one of the artist's most discussed pieces, depicting in extreme close-up the narrowed eyes of a helmeted super-villain (the original inspiration is a panel from the first issue of Marvel's *X-Men* series, drawn by Jack Kirby, and the malefactor in question is the X-Men's archfoe Magneto). The huge dialogue balloon that fills the upper half of the canvas reads, "What?

Why did you ask that? What do you know about my Image Duplicator?"

This is not the original dialogue from the comic book source, and the meaning of the words is apparent: although the villain seems to be referring to some sci-fi doomsday machine, the "Image Duplicator" is actually the artist himself. The dialogue is a tongue-in-cheek reference to Lichtenstein's style, and the interrogatory tone ("What do you know . . .") seems to be a rebuke to closed-minded critics. In a sense, *Image Duplicator* is a kind of self-portrait—a linguistic one rather than a strict visual representation.

Lichtenstein and all the rest were the darlings of much of the art world, and even New York's social scene was affected by the movement. Andy Warhol, the most visible of the group (and the most canny self-promoter) established the place that became the "in" destination for the city's avant-garde set throughout the 1960s, the Factory, initially located at 231 East 47th Street. Originally a studio space for Warhol, the Factory became a Pop Art legend in its own right, and a New York institution.

6

BEYOND COMICS

ART ABOUT ART

The 1960s were well suited to the rise of Pop Art, which was reaching its zenith by the beginning of 1964. The button-down attitude of the 1950s, which had carried into the early years of the decade, was largely a quaint memory by the mid-1960s. The assassination of President Kennedy in November 1963 shocked the nation and sparked a change in the national mood. The Vietnam conflict was ramping up, and America became more embroiled in it as the new president, Lyndon Johnson, reinstituted the draft. Opposition to the controversial war was growing on the home front, and the civil rights struggles, personified by figures such as Rosa Parks and the Reverend Martin Luther King Jr., were threatening to tear apart the foundations of the nation. The Civil Rights Bill was passed in 1964, but by the end of the decade, both Robert Kennedy and Reverend King would join JFK on the list of national heroes felled by assassins' bullets. Throughout it all, the momentous march of pop continued: the fictional universe of NBC's *Star Trek* promised a brighter future without prejudice and heralded the landmark *Apollo 11* moon landing in 1969. America had truly entered the space age.

New York, as usual, was in the eye of the social and cultural storm: 1964 saw the Beatles' first performance in America (at New York's Ed Sullivan Theater, today the site of CBS's *Late Show*), bringing the British Invasion into homes across the country. That same year, antiwar protestors marched in the streets of Gotham, and the World's Fair was held in Queens. In 1969, the Stonewall Inn riots in Greenwich Village galvanized the gay rights movement.

With his city and the world changing rapidly around him, Roy Lichtenstein's art was changing as well. Just as New York's most significant event of the time—the 1964 World's Fair—was introducing Pop Art to the world at large, the man who had been largely responsible for the movement was gradually leaving behind the subject matter that had been his bread and butter for three years. By 1965, comic book panels had largely disappeared from his work in favor of an assortment of new subjects, all of which were personal, made a specific statement, and were done in the now-familiar style that Lichtenstein had appropriated as distinctly his own. He was ready to apply his touch to the art that had truly inspired him as a youth, and to the unique architecture of the city that had welcomed him back with open arms and showered him with long-awaited success.

DISSECTING THE POP PHENOMENON

Perhaps a nation facing the challenges of the late 1960s simply needed art that did not take itself too seriously, art that laid bare the consumerist society that America had become. Pop Art, and popular culture in general, inspired numerous analyses by the cognoscenti of the era. John Canaday posed the provocative question, "Pop Art Sells On and On—Why?" as the title of a May 31, 1964, article for the *New York Times Magazine*. Without reaching a definitive conclusion, Canaday touches on the notion that the "Popists" (as Andy Warhol dubbed them in an autobiography) were making statements on the decline of culture itself:

> As the New landscape, Pop is proving once more that nature imitates art. Where Pop used to look like comic strips or highway restaurant signs, highway restaurant signs and comic strips are beginning to look like Pop, which is an improvement of sorts. . . . A theory is that Pop Art is the artist's solution—and through him, ours—to living in the world as it is. All the horrendousness of contemporary life—the mass-produced objects devoid of taste, the degraded images produced serially by the hundreds of thousands—must be not only accepted but embraced. By accepting and even by exaggerating these horrors, we have at least the form of escape involved in the adage, "If you can't lick 'em, join 'em."

When asked about his feelings about the subjects he was addressing in his art, Lichtenstein rarely said anything more incendiary than his quote that was used to close a

1964 *Life* magazine profile: "I'm in favor of these things as subject matter, but not as social condition."

GLIMPSING THE FUTURE IN QUEENS

New York announced itself loudly as the world's cultural leader in 1964 with the New York World's Fair, held in Flushing Meadows Park in the borough of Queens, today the site of Citi Field, home of the New York Mets (as well as Citi Field's predecessor, the now-demolished Shea Stadium) and the USTA National Tennis Center, host of the US Open. The area had been a massive garbage dump until the 1930s, when one of New York's most famous master architects, Robert Moses, tried to use the 1939 World's Fair to create a vast recreational facility on nearly 900 acres at Flushing Meadows. The fair did not generate the finances needed to finish the project he'd envisioned, and Moses saw the 1964 fair as a chance to finish what he'd started.

The 1964 World's Fair was mired in controversy. Many of the fair organizers' plans, such as charging rent to exhibitors and holding the fair for two years rather than the usual one, were against the regulations of the Bureau of International Exhibitors (BIE), the body that sanctions world's fairs. Moses and the organizers brushed off the BIE's objections and went ahead with their plans without the bureau's blessing (the United States was not a BIE member nation), ensuring that participation by other nations would be minimal.

Philip Johnson: Pop Architect

One of the major figures in twentieth-century American architecture, Philip Johnson's influence on New York, as both an architect and a patron of the arts, is still felt today. Johnson's purchase of Lichtenstein's *Girl with Ball* was a watershed moment in the artist's career and put Pop Art on the map for New York's savviest art collectors. Much like Lichtenstein, Johnson made his reputation by breaking the conventional standards of his field, and in doing so left an indelible imprint on the city of New York.

Born to a wealthy family in Cleveland, Ohio, on July 8, 1906, Johnson graduated from Harvard in 1930 with a degree in philosophy and quickly afterward became director of the Department of Architecture at the Museum of Modern Art. In this role, he introduced many Americans to the European style of modern architecture pioneered by such figures as Le Corbusier, Walter Gropius, and Ludwig Mies van der Rohe, all of whom in turn influenced Johnson's own work as an architect.

His most prolific period was the 1950s, when he collaborated with Mies van der Rohe on the landmark Seagram Building on Park Avenue, meshing elements of classical architecture with contemporary, Modernist styles. He was still producing major works in the 1980s, designing (often with Richard Foster, his collaborator on the New York State Pavilion) such New York mainstays as 550 Madison Avenue, formerly the Sony Building and AT&T Building; Tisch Hall at New York University; the Paley Center for Media, formerly the

Museum of Television and Radio, at West 52nd Street; and the David H. Koch Theater, formerly the New York State Theater. In Pop Art, Johnson saw painters turning artistic conventions on their heads much as he was doing with the rules of building design. It was only natural that this architectural iconoclast would use the stage of the 1964 World's Fair to display the work of America's newest artistic stars.

As a result, the 1964 fair was mostly a showcase for American industry, business, and popular culture. Visitors to Flushing Meadows from April 1964 to October 1965 were treated to a glimpse of the so-called space age. The General Motors *Futurama* exhibit offered visitors a tour in moving armchairs, which glided past dioramas depicting the world of the future. Walt Disney unveiled "audio-animatronics"—computer-operated lifelike robots that today are standard among the exhibits at Disney theme parks. President Kennedy, who had broken ground for the federal government's pavilion in 1962, was honored in several exhibits. Individual states made contributions, such as Wisconsin's "World's Largest Cheese," Florida's porpoise show with water skiers, and Illinois's animatronic, speech-making Abe Lincoln. The state of New York, not to be outdone, hosted the $6 million "Tent of Tomorrow," designed by architect Philip Johnson and featuring murals by ten Pop artists, including Lichtenstein, Warhol, Rosenquist, Rauschenberg, and Indiana. Johnson had commissioned Lichtenstein to do a mural, the artist's first large-scale work, back in early 1963.

The 1964 World's Fair was an eminently suitable stage for Pop Art. Warhol, always a lightning rod for controversy, received the most attention with his *Thirteen Most Wanted Men*, which featured huge photos of criminals (mostly Italian mafiosi) on the FBI's most wanted list. Johnson insisted Warhol remove the work for fear of offending his Italian clients. Warhol responded with an alternative even more likely to draw ire: twenty-five identical silk-screened portraits of a sinister-looking Robert Moses. Johnson also rejected that idea, and ultimately kept Warhol's criminal portraits on the mural, albeit nearly obscured by a coat of silver paint.

Apolitical as usual, Lichtenstein's contribution to the fair was a massive image of a pretty redheaded girl straight out of a romance comic leaning out of a window. He also was commissioned to do the cover for the April 1964 issue of *Art in America*, a complex pop panorama illustration that depicts many of the fair's futuristic exhibits.

In the end, the 1964 World's Fair was a money-losing endeavor, unable to repay its many creditors and embroiled in legal disputes with them until 1970, when the books were closed and the World's Fair Corporation dissolved. Moses's vision for Flushing Meadows was never fully realized, and only a few symbols of the fair remain, notably the massive Unisphere, the representation of a space age Earth embodying the event's motto, "Man's Achievements on a Shrinking Globe in an Expanding Universe." The former New York State Pavilion is an abandoned and neglected relic. The fair's Space Park is part of the New York Hall of Science, displaying rockets and other vehicles used in America's history of space exploration. Fittingly for the site of the World's Fair that enshrined the masters of Pop Art, the Queens Museum has found a home there, in the former New York City building. A multimillion-dollar model of the city is among its exhibits.

As for Roy Lichtenstein, he was none the worse for wear after the World's Fair wrapped up. His mural, along with the nine others, was de-installed in October of 1965, and Lichtenstein's first large-scale work today resides at the University of Minnesota.

NO SUCH THING AS BAD PUBLICITY

The World's Fair was one of many milestones for Lichtenstein in 1964. In the sixties, a profile in *Life* magazine was a good indication that an artist had "made it." Even so, any excitement Lichtenstein may have felt about being featured in the January 31, 1964, issue must have been tempered somewhat by the article's title: "Is He the Worst Artist in the US?" An echo of the magazine's 1949 article on Jackson Pollock ("Is He the Greatest Living Painter in the US?"), the feature was actually a balanced look at Lichtenstein, his work, and the accusations of his critics. The author, Dorothy Seiberling, asked Lichtenstein directly about the critics' main point of contention: whether he directly copied his source material or whether he transformed it into something else, and whether that something else was, in fact, art. "The closer my work is to the original," he replied, "the more threatening the content. . . . I take a cliché and try to organize its forms to make it monumental. The difference is often not great but it is crucial."

Art Grows in the Bowery

New York's infamous hard-luck alley and boulevard of broken dreams, the one-mile stretch in the East Village called the Bowery, took its name from the Dutch word for "farm"—*bouwerij*—referring to the farm of the land's original owner, Peter Stuyvesant, in 1651. Throughout the fascinating history of New York, this area has played a significant role.

When New York was still a Dutch colony called New Amsterdam in the 1700s, the road was used to drive cattle. At the end of the American Revolution, the defeated British soldiers were marched down the Bowery as they retreated to England. In the early nineteenth century, the area came alive with fashionable entertainment spots such as the Bowery Theater and the raucous "pleasure resorts" such as Vauxhall Gardens (on the block that now houses the offices of the *Village Voice*). As with other "hot" New York neighborhoods then and now, wealthy investors (such as Jacob Astor, after whom the Village street Astor Place is named) bought land and eventually moved out, leaving the neighborhood to the working poor and the expanding masses of immigrants. It is these people who came to be known as Bowery boys and gals.

Not long after its heyday, the Bowery became known for poverty, gang violence, and various forms of sin and sleaze. Near the corner of Bowery and Houston Street was a bar known as McGurk's Suicide

Hall, where an inordinate number of prostitutes killed themselves. The early Chinese settlers established bordellos and opium dens, drawing curious visitors. Rival gangs of "dead-end" kids engaged in brawls and riots. At one point it got so bad that the residents of the northern stretch between Cooper Square and Union Square successfully lobbied to have the name of their area changed from Bowery to 4th Avenue, as it remains today. The Great Depression was regarded as the nadir of the neighborhood, inspiring novels, movies, and songs that established the "skid row" image of rummy bars and flophouses that lingers today. In the 1950s and 1960s, low rents and the "outsider" image attracted New York's artistic community to the storied neighborhood.

Inspiration Old and New

Despite his status as an art world cause célèbre in 1964, critics' warming to the value of his work, and the enormous financial success that he was finally enjoying (Seiberling's *Life* profile cited that his canvases were selling for as much as $4,000 each by that point), Lichtenstein continued to explore new subject matter. Leo Castelli and Ivan Karp were willing to indulge just about any whim of Lichtenstein's at that point—his paintings were making the gallery a great deal of money—and they showed several of Lichtenstein's new works in an exhibition in October and November 1964, giving the artist's devotees and detractors alike more to mull over, discuss, and debate.

Followers of Lichtenstein's art during the early 1960s were also treated to his first works that explored another type of subject matter—representations of works by artists such as Picasso and Cézanne, all executed in Lichtenstein's now-familiar trademark style. If some critics are apoplectic over huge, blown-up images out of the comic strips, Lichtenstein may have slyly asked himself, what are they going to think about representations of famous fine art paintings or classical architecture, all done in that same mechanical, commercialized style—thick outlines, four-color dots, and all?

In 1964, New York City began to play a more direct role in inspiring Lichtenstein's artwork. Like any kid who grew up in the city, Lichtenstein had spent a large portion of his youth riding the subway, and he became intrigued by the enameled signs that adorned the underground stations. He began making enameled steel sculptures, utilizing the services of a New Jersey firm called Architectural Porcelain to fabricate the pieces. *Clouds and Sea* (1964) is an example of these pieces, as are the editioned prints of *Ten Landscapes* (1967), a portfolio of screen prints using industrial materials such as Rowlux.

Lichtenstein had not totally abandoned his comic strip muses in 1964, and a series he did that year centered around the theme of women in danger or distress—crying, fretting, frightened, and mostly in extreme close-up. Lichtenstein, despite his offhanded speculation later on that his impending divorce "might have" had an influence on his subject matter, always maintained that he kept the same clinical distance from the emotional content of these paintings that he did from all the others. In fact, he claimed to be fascinated by the dichotomy itself—the overwrought emotionalism depicted in a dispassionate manner, the opposite of the raw emotion conveyed by the wild brushstrokes of a van Gogh, an Edvard Munch, or a Jackson Pollock. "They were usually clichés about the emotionalism of women," he told *Harper's Bazaar*, "but then I was interested in emotion whether it was war or whether it was women."

The "women" paintings generated just as much controversy in years to come as the "war" paintings, and for the same reason: the lack of credit to and compensation for the comic book artists whose panels were being appropriated, among them such industry greats as Tony Abruzzo, Ted Galindo, and John Romita Sr. The controversy has yet to die down, as illustrrated by this 2015 news article in the sci-fi/fantasy magazine *Heavy Metal*:

> Lichtenstein, as dictated by his pop art aesthetic, took everyday images and inserted them into the highbrow art world, and was celebrated for it. Yet he wasn't taking, as Warhol did, corporate imagery like a Brillo Pads box or a Campbell's soup can. Lichtenstein was taking—copying, often exactly—images created by contemporary working artists. John Romita draws a frame in the '60s—one frame out of a comic book that runs for dozens of pages—and is compensated modestly for it. Lichtenstein copies Romita's frame and it commands thousands, later millions of dollars. It's hung in fancy galleries and museums. Is John Romita cited for his original work? No.

If Roy Lichtenstein was indeed dealing with emotional issues over his impending divorce in his 1964 women paintings, he reached a turning point by autumn of that year.

Making preparations for the *American Supermarket* exhibition, he made the acquaintance of the woman who would share the rest of his life.

THE GIRL FROM
THE SUPERMARKET

In 1964, Dorothy Herzka was the director of the Paul Bianchini Gallery (16 E. 78th Street), one block south of Leo Castelli's, which had hosted Lichtenstein's career-making sold-out show in 1962. Blonde, with all-American good looks, Dorothy could almost have been a romance comic "girl in distress" in a Lichtenstein painting. Charged with devising art shows for Bianchini that showed more of a contemporary edge, Dorothy scheduled the *American Supermarket* show.

This exhibition was a unique type of art show, even for the heyday of Pop: the gallery was set up like a grocery store, with items for sale that were also original works of art: Warhol soup cans; a 3-D turkey by Tom Wesselman; sculptures of cakes, cookies, and candies by Oldenburg; plaster loaves of bread by Robert Watts; and, presumably for gallery goers to carry purchases home, shopping bags emblazoned with screen prints of a cartoon turkey by Lichtenstein and a Campbell's soup can by Warhol.

A CHANGE OF SCENERY

Lichtenstein's ever-evolving painting style underwent some alterations in 1964, both in the studio process and in the finished product that hung in the galleries. The store-bought metal screens he was using to apply the Ben-Day dots to his paintings were replaced with paper screens that the artist had made especially for him. Lichtenstein began making his dots larger, in proportion to the dimensions of each painting. He also abandoned one of his standard motifs—the comic strip dialogue balloons began appearing with less frequency and disappeared altogether by 1966. On June 30, 1964, Lichtenstein resigned his teaching position at Douglass College to concentrate fully on his career as an artist.

Lichtenstein was mentally about as far from the dreary struggles and failing marriage of his Oswego days as he could get. He officially separated from Isabel in 1965, and the divorce was finalized in 1967, with Isabel gaining custody of their two children. (Roy would largely take over their raising soon afterward, however, when Isabel became incapacitated by an illness. She died, relatively young, in 1980.) He was no longer doing odd jobs to make ends meet, and he was making art for a living instead of teaching it. Most significantly, he was back in the heart of New York City's most artistic, bohemian enclave, having moved from his studio on West 26th Street to a nine-room warehouse in the Bowery.

The building he moved into in 1966, 190 Bowery, was a former German bank, built in the late 1800s and located under the decrepit ruins of an elevated subway line that had been shut down in 1955. Among the other residents of the huge converted warehouse were artists Mark Rothko, Malcolm Morley, Adolph Gottlieb, and Louise Nevelson.

Factory Follies: Inside Pop Art's 1960s Palace

Despite the envy that Andy Warhol exhibited after Lichtenstein "scooped" him on Mickey Mouse and beat him to Castelli's representation, the two titans of Pop Art were friends, admiring and collecting each other's work (Warhol even did a portrait of Lichtenstein in 1975). On the social scene, they were mostly polar opposites—Lichtenstein enjoyed quiet and solitude, while Warhol became a fixture in New York's legendary nightlife. On occasion, however, especially after beginning his relationship with Dorothy, Lichtenstein made an appearance at his colleague's ultra-hip studio/party space.

During the 1960s, there was no cooler place to see and be seen in New York City than the Factory, Andy Warhol's art studio, which became renowned as a decadent nightlife hangout for artists, celebrities, and social misfits of all stripes. The three-pronged 1960s cliché of sex, drugs, and rock 'n' roll was a nightly reality there, drawing regular patrons such as Bob Dylan, Truman Capote, Rudolf Nureyev, John Lennon, Mick Jagger, David Bowie, and Lou Reed. Warhol, in addition to producing paintings, prints, and filmmaking projects, also became the manager of Reed's influential band, the Velvet Underground; Reed's solo classic "Walk on the Wild Side" was inspired by the transvestites, amphetamine addicts, and other assorted characters he met at the Factory.

During the Factory's heyday, in the Pop-ascendant years of 1963 to 1967, the Factory was at 231 East

47th Street, in the heart of midtown, which at the time held most of the city's art galleries. The Factory's decor reflected its eccentric proprietor: walls covered with tinfoil and silver paint, with big, helium-filled, pillow-shaped balloons functioning as silver clouds on the ceiling.

In addition to the famous people sighted there, the Factory created some of its own celebrities (or "superstars," as Warhol called them), most notably the original "Factory Girl," model Edie Sedgwick. A free-spirited heiress with stunning features, a drop-dead slender figure, and an eyebrow-raising avant-garde fashion sense, Sedgwick became a 1960s pop culture icon. She and Warhol—who had a Pygmalion-like relationship with her—were regarded as the city's reigning "Pop Couple." She became so famous as Warhol's muse, and her style so recognizable, that at a Halloween party in 1964, Dorothy Herzka, who was dating Lichtenstein, dressed up as Sedgwick, sporting hot pants, high heels, and silver glitter. Roy was at her side, dressed, of course, as Warhol.

It wasn't all parties and debauchery at the Factory, however. One of New York's most notorious events of the Pop era took place there on June 3, 1968, when Valerie Solanas, a militant feminist and aspiring playwright who had performed in several of Warhol's films, walked into the studio in broad daylight and fired three bullets at the unsuspecting artist and two of his guests. Solanas calmly walked out and turned herself in to police, claiming that Warhol was trying to steal her work and that he "had too much control over my life." In the end, she pleaded guilty (Warhol did not testify against her) and received three years in prison. Warhol, whose spleen, stomach, liver, and esophagus were torn up by the close-range shot, never fully recovered from the attack, and had to wear a corset for the rest of his life. The incident was dramatized in the 1998 film *I Shot Andy Warhol*.

The popularity of the Factory—enhanced by the buzz surrounding Pop Art—anticipated the notoriety of Studio 54 in the 1970s, brought about by the disco music and dance craze. Many of the Factory's faithful became frequent patrons of 54 as well.

The writer William Burroughs lived in the neighborhood, as well as Debbie Harry of the punk band Blondie, who would find fame, along with many of her contemporaries, at a run-down club called CBGB's, up the street at Bowery and 2nd Street, which opened in 1973.

Lichtenstein's years in his Bowery studio would inspire some of his most interesting work, and it seems that after years of being on the outside of the movement he had helped launch—commuting from Cleveland, from Oswego, even from the relative closeness of New Jersey—he finally felt truly in his element. Initially attracted to the building by its low cost and plentiful space, Lichtenstein was inspired by its location at the center of the artistic action and by being among creative neighbors who were redefining popular culture in their own way.

Batman: Pop Conquers the Small Screen

Unlike Andy Warhol, Roy Lichtenstein never seriously entered the field of filmmaking. However, if a Lichtenstein painting from the early 1960s had been translated into a live-action program, it probably would have looked a lot like ABC's *Batman*, the hit television series that introduced millions of American viewers to the word—and concept—of "camp."

Based on the successful DC Comics series, the show made its debut on January 12, 1966, and starred Adam West as the title character and Burt Ward as his youthful sidekick, Robin, the Boy Wonder. A host of veteran character actors appeared on the show as costumed villains, most notably Cesar Romero as the cackling "Clown Prince of Crime," the Joker; Burgess Meredith as the waddling, umbrella-toting Penguin; Frank Gorshin as the puzzle-obsessed Riddler; and Julie Newmar as the slinky, seductive Catwoman. Part of the show's almost-instant popularity was due to its unique format, with two half-hour episodes airing on consecutive nights, the first one a cliffhanger leading into the other. The show's "campy" attitude—with its mock-serious dialogue, cheeky cultural references, pompous voice-over narration, and double entendres—made it must-see viewing for millions of devotees during the Pop Art era. Perhaps its most lasting cultural contribution was the use of onomatopoeic cartoon sound effects ("Pow!" "Bam!" "Whapp!") bursting onto the screen, usually at a point of impact, such as a fist hitting a face or a chair breaking over someone's back, during the program's fight scenes. A device once familiar only to comic book readers, its use in *Batman* brought it into general usage, particularly among those writing about comics and Pop Art. Because Lichtenstein was the Pop Artist most identified with comics, many a treatise on his work includes a "Pow" or "Blam" as part of its title. Of course, Lichtenstein discovered the kitschy appeal of these bombastic lettered sound effects years before, particularly in his war scene paintings.

The writers and producers of *Batman* were not unaware of their place in the reign of Pop. In the second season, the show paid tribute to the art of the 1960s in an episode called "Pop Goes the Joker." The plot revolved around the villain's clever scheme to defraud art collectors by passing off meaningless scribbles as priceless paintings.

Many serious comic book fans, used to the traditional image of Batman as a hard-edged, film noir–esque "creature of the night" character, disdained the show's irreverent, tongue-in-cheek take on their hero—echoing the attitude of many art critics about Pop Art's skewering of artistic conventions—but they were in the minority. The show was a ratings smash for three years and spawned an explosion of *Batman* licensed merchandise that ranged from toys, games, puzzles, and plastic models to lunchboxes, toothbrushes, and tableware. Perhaps due to overexposure, the ratings dropped as quickly as they had risen, and the show was canceled in 1968. Although it helped popularize comics in the 1960s, the program's long-term effects were more harmful than helpful to the medium.

It would be years before adults in the United States would see comics as anything other than outmoded, silly artifacts of a more simplistic era—long after Roy Lichtenstein had abandoned his interest in them.

THINKING IN 3-D

Although the traditional war and romance images were working their way out of Lichtenstein's painting repertoire by the end of 1965, the comics were still providing fodder for some of his other experimentations, particularly in sculpture. Lichtenstein began using 3-D media such as ceramics to create radical versions of colorful 2-D subject matter.

He tried his hand at sculptures, such as *Small Explosion*, using the cartoon representations of smoke, fire, and violence as his source material, but he soon focused on a series of *Head* sculptures, for which he enlisted the aid of ceramicist Hui Ka Kwong. Lichtenstein had actually created the prototype of this sculpture series the previous year, while still at his apartment and studio on West 26th Street, in the heart of what was then New York's hat manufacturing district. Once again finding inspiration in the mundane trappings of everyday Manhattan life, Lichtenstein snapped up a few of the plentiful plaster mannequins in the local shops and painted one of them up to resemble a romantic comic book heroine, naming the piece *Head of Girl*. He took this idea a few steps further in 1965, creating sculptural, realistic ceramic heads with female features, and adding his distinct graphic touches to establish an ambiguous sense of form and shadow. The results of the collaboration with Kwong were ten pieces (four unfinished), each with different-colored shadow areas, simply dubbed *Head with Red Shadow*, *Head with Blue Shadow*, *Head with Black Shadow*, and so on.

an evening with the popists

As the 1960s were reaching their midpoint, Pop Art had evolved from an art world phenomenon to a mainstream success, and the Pop artists of New York had gone from quirky, avant-garde personalities celebrated on the Manhattan art scene to legitimate, nationally known celebrities.

One sign that the movement had truly arrived was the publication in 1965 of the first book devoted exclusively to the subject: *Pop Art*, written by John Rublowski with photography by Ken Heyman. The launch party, held at Andy Warhol's Factory (231 E. 47th Street), was a veritable VIP summit for the Pop masters and a gaggle of guests, more than three hundred in all. The party—thrown by the publisher, Basic Books—was seen by some in the media as more a wake than a celebration, since the white-hot popularity of the movement was already cooling. Nevertheless, it was a memorable event.

Held in a notoriously hot, stuffy, non-air-conditioned space (a guest of honor, Oldenburg, referred to the room as "Andy's Turkish Bath"), the party featured beer and hot dogs from a pushcart vendor (a kitsch menu, indeed), rock music by a band called the Denims, and besotted patrons attempting the frug and watusi, the hot dances of the time.

Lichtenstein was reportedly one of the few who appeared cool and comfortable among the legions of overheated guests who'd shed jackets and ties for T-shirts. A *New York Times* reporter covering the party asked Lichtenstein if Pop Art was dead. "No, I don't see any signs of pop art being dead," was his measured but definitive response. "But . . . it's taking a different direction." If he wasn't speaking for the entire Pop movement, he was certainly describing his own part in it.

COMMISSIONED WORKS

Lichtenstein respected fine art and took exception to the notion that the work he produced should be considered anything but. However, he was also a practical man raising a family, a man who treated every day in the studio like a day at the office. It should be no surprise, then—especially considering his extensive experience in commercial illustration—that he began to take on commissioned work for a variety of clients, including cover illustrations for some of the most prestigious New York–based magazine publishers.

The April 25, 1966, issue of *Newsweek* featured an article called "The Story of Pop: What It Is and How It Came to Be." Lichtenstein was hired to do the cover illustration. The story focused on the emerging societal trends that seemed to be directly or indirectly influenced by Pop Art, such as the nostalgic interest in 1930s movies and movie poster art; the new fascination with trivia; increasingly aggressive and unconventional trends in advertising; the "new dandy" aesthetic in fashion, owing partly to Britain's famous Carnaby Street look; and the growing ubiquity of comic book superheroes in media, entertainment, and licensed products, from the Broadway musical featuring Superman to the smash-hit *Batman* television series.

In addition to the *Newsweek* cover illustration, the other major commissioned work that Lichtenstein undertook in 1966 was a poster for the Fourth New York Film Festival, held at Lincoln Center. The poster's design evoked images of Hollywood's 1930s golden age, with its bright primary colors, elegant typography, and art deco touches.

The New York Film Festival began at Lincoln Center in 1963, intended as a showcase for important films that might not otherwise be seen by large audiences in the United States. The fourth festival opened on September 12, 1966, at Lincoln Center's Philharmonic Hall, and featured a lineup of mostly foreign films. Twenty-four feature-length films were screened over the two-week festival, including commercial studio films, student films, underground and avant-garde pieces, and examples of the new documentary style known as cinema verité. The Pop sensibility of the 1960s also made its presence known. The festival—whose stated focus was on "films of the future"—showed a number of innovative television commercials, which were being acknowledged as having a growing influence on filmmakers. The appreciation of independent and foreign films was a new thing in the 1960s, and another sign of a growing counterculture zeitgeist looking for forms of entertainment that were a bit more edgy and dangerous than the typical fare being churned out by the large Hollywood studios.

CHRONICLING CHAOS

Andy Warhol was not the most famous person shot in 1968. On April 4, Martin Luther King Jr. was assassinated in Memphis, Tennessee, at the hands of an ex-convict from a Mississippi penitentiary named James Earl Ray. The nation barely had time to recover from this blow when Robert Kennedy, making a bid for the presidency, was gunned down after finishing a speech at Los Angeles's Ambassador Hotel on June 5. The assailant was a Jordanian-American named Sirhan Bishara Sirhan, though, like JFK's assassination in 1963, the circumstances were bizarre and left open the possibility of a larger conspiracy. A sense of fear and frustration was becoming predominant throughout America. With his once-reviled, eminently recognizable art style becoming more and more mainstream, Lichtenstein was a natural choice to produce covers for New York's top newsweeklies in a year that was marked by one national crisis after another.

Just two weeks before RFK's fateful appointment in Los Angeles, the May 24 issue of *Time* sported a commissioned Lichtenstein portrait of the presidential candidate on its cover. The Kennedy portrait, done in felt-tip markers over graphite on matte board, now resides in the Smithsonian Institution's National Portrait Gallery in Washington, DC. A similar theme—gun violence in America—no doubt inspired by the tragic deaths of both RFK and MLK, as well as the previous year's race riots in Detroit, was evident in another Lichtenstein magazine cover, the June 21 cover of *Time*. The feature story, "The Gun in America," was illustrated by Lichtenstein's simple rendering of a hand holding a smoking pistol. As usual, the artist's commercial art shorthand for a complex, serious subject spoke volumes.

Because these pieces were both commissioned works, it is difficult to know if Lichtenstein was making any personal social statement through them. But his masterpiece of 1968, the intriguingly titled *Preparedness*, leaves little room for doubt. Measuring 10 feet high by 8 feet wide, with three distinct panels, *Preparedness* adopts the techniques of Fernand Léger and the WPA artists of the 1930s—known for their massive murals that depicted the plight of the working class—to portray what is regarded by many as an ironic statement on the military-industrial complex. With its Cubist-inspired collage of futuristic-looking machinery and anonymous, expressionless, identical soldiers, the painting appears to be commenting on the loss of humanity and identity that comes with becoming a cog in the proverbial "war machine." The theme of *Preparedness* was certainly appropriate for its time. The nation was deeply divided in 1968, as the wounds of the Vietnam War and the civil rights struggle seemed to cut more deeply by the month. *Preparedness* now hangs in the Guggenheim Museum.

The year was also memorable in another way: Roy Lichtenstein and Dorothy Herzka managed to carve out their own little piece of happiness in the midst of the nation's dark days; they were married on November 4.

HISTORY AT THE GUGGENHEIM

As a turbulent decade drew to a close, Roy Lichtenstein received a singular honor—the first New York retrospective of his work, which opened on September 19, 1969, at one of the city's most renowned showplaces of modern and contemporary art, the Solomon R. Guggenheim Museum (5th Avenue at 89th Street).

The foundations for this landmark museum were laid in the late 1920s, when industrialist Solomon R. Guggenheim hired a spiritual "non-objectivist" painter named Hilla Rebay as his chief art adviser; Guggenheim established his eponymous foundation in 1937. In 1939, Guggenheim founded the Museum of Non-Objective Painting in a former automobile showroom on East 54th Street, with Rebay as its director. The museum was dedicated to cutting-edge artistic styles from the outset: its opening exhibit, echoing the themes of the 1939 World's Fair, was *The Art of Tomorrow*, featuring the radical work of European pioneers such as Wassily Kandinsky, Paul Klee, and Piet Mondrian. In 1959, the Museum of Non-Objective Painting was given a permanent home and was rechristened the Solomon R. Guggenheim Museum.

Frank Lloyd Wright was enlisted to design the building; the structure would become one of Wright's last great projects. The architect conceived the Guggenheim as a "temple of spirit" that would offer visitors an entirely new way of looking at art. The circular design, with its curving, continuous gallery halls, rebelled against the rectilinear grid of Manhattan. Wright was quite proud of his achievement, telling *Architectural Digest*, "Entering into the spirit of the interior, you will discover the best possible atmosphere in which to show fine paintings or listen to music. It is this atmosphere that seems to me most lacking in our art galleries, museums, music halls, and theaters." The crowds that greeted its opening in 1959, and the throngs that visit to this day, indicate that New York's art lovers agreed. The Guggenheim Museum is generally regarded as one of the great architectural works of the twentieth century.

In addition to *Preparedness*, several important works by Lichtenstein reside in the Guggenheim's permanent collection, including *Grrrrrrrrrr!!* (1965), with its image of an aggressive, growling dog; the Surrealist *Girl with Tear I* (1977); one of the 1976 *Entablature* works; the 1960s painted-brass sculpture *Modern Sculpture with Three Discs;* and *Interior with Mirrored Wall* (1991), from his late-period *Interiors* series.

The eyes of the art critics were trained on Lichtenstein's landmark show at the Guggenheim, which included more than one hundred paintings, sculptures, drawings, and ceramics. Although it seemed the Pop Art craze was receding to the back of the cultural consciousness, appreciation of Lichtenstein's work was beginning to become more widespread—in part, perhaps, because this show finally made it clear to the critics that not only was Lichtenstein able to create work beyond the comic strip medium, but that he and his work were not going away anytime soon.

Defining 1969 "as the year pop art came of age or as the year that it died," John Canaday reviewed the Guggenheim exhibit for the *New York Times*. His review focused on the growth in the artist's style that the show displayed. "Speaking as one vulgarian to another, I think you will enjoy Mr. Lichtenstein's Guggenheim show if you take it at its face value," Canaday wrote in the September 20, 1969, edition:

It begins with those earliest paintings where Mr. Lichtenstein stuck so closely to the style of comic strips that his
enlargements included some of the fuzziness and blotting
of the Ben Day process areas as printed on cheap paper.
Shortly, however, Mr. Lichtenstein began working in the
very precise manner that now identifies him; the dots
grew larger and were disposed with immaculate clarity
and regularity. . . . As he has gone on and on, Mr. Lichtenstein has been more and more attentive to this impersonal, mechanistic manner. It gives his work a perverse
elegance.

Canaday offered further thoughts on the retrospective, and Lichtenstein's growth as an artist, in the following
day's Arts section. "His first exhibitions in the early 1960s,
as everyone remembers, were of enlarged frames of comic
strips, complete with balloons filled with the godawfulest
kind of comic strip language," he wrote:

Currently [he] is riding the tide of a revived interest in the
1930s by doing with the decorative styles of that decade
what he used to do with the comics, and we are told that
we must not call him a pop artist any more. . . . These
pseudo-30s pieces . . . were vulgar enough to begin with,
as a matter of fact, with that special kind of vulgarity that
the French so often confuse with high style. In passing
through Mr. Lichtenstein's slicking-up mill the motifs become doubly vulgar. On the principle that a double negative makes a positive, perhaps one could argue that Mr.
Lichtenstein has given them a new elegance.

Another Times critic, Grace Glueck, visited Lichtenstein and his wife in the Bowery loft studio at the kickoff of
the Guggenheim exhibit, noting the presence of assistants

applying dots to several large canvases. Glueck's interview offers insight into the tongue-in-cheek quality of Lichtenstein's work that had escaped so many of his harsher critics. "I had a thing about clichés," he admitted. "I suddenly thought, why not do a whole cartoon? I started out just to see what it would look like, but then I got serious about the formal relationships. Maybe I was also making fun of the 'precious' quality of art. I wanted to get ha-ha humor in it."

Glueck described Lichtenstein as "a slim, mild-mannered fellow as modest as they come (in the New York art world)"—a description that would be echoed by many who knew him over the years. Lichtenstein proved the impression true with an oft-repeated mantra that he put forth in the article: "I couldn't have done it, though," he said, "if certain things weren't in the air." The statement was a subtle nod to all that had made his experimentation possible—Kaprow's Happenings, Johns's *Flag* series, Oldenburg's sculptural food, Rauschenberg's Coke bottles, and even the creative trails blazed by the New York School in the years after World War II—even while it was all fading into history. The 1970s were dawning, and new and different "things" were in the air. Lichtenstein's work, as always, would reflect them.

7

MIRRORS, INDIANS, AND THE NEXT GENERATION

NEW FRONTIERS IN THE SEVENTIES

As the 1970s began, the nation was nursing a hangover from the late 1960s. The war in Vietnam was still raging as the decade dawned, though it would come to its ignominious end in 1975. Another national scandal, Watergate, was boiling to the surface in Washington and would ultimately lead to the resignation of embattled president Richard M. Nixon in 1974. The public's disillusionment helped elect Democrat Jimmy Carter to the presidency over Nixon's successor, Gerald Ford, in 1976. Carter's term, however, was not the tonic for the national morale that some had hoped. Inflation spiraled out of control throughout the decade, and the 1973 oil embargo led to long lines at the

Pop on the Block: The Golden Age of Art Auctions

In a stunning contrast to the overall economic malaise that gripped New York in the 1970s, the auction market for art in general—and Pop Art in particular—was white-hot throughout the decade, a trend that would continue into the materialistic 1980s. In New York's prestigious auction houses, Lichtenstein and his Pop contemporaries commanded historic prices from collectors who were, perhaps, realizing that the sun had set on the movement and the works that remained were now a part of American art history.

October 18, 1973, was a watershed moment for the business of auctioning art, and it was the once-reviled Pop masters who were in the driver's seat. Robert Scull and his wife, Ethel, owners of a private fleet of taxicabs, were among the most prolific collectors of Pop Art in the 1960s, and in 1973 they decided to put a substantial part of their collection, including several early Lichtensteins, up for auction at Sotheby's, one of the world's most prestigious auction houses.

The 1973 Scull auction featured fifty Pop Art masterpieces and drew a packed house of dealers, collectors, and other artists, who arrived in such droves that they had to be admitted in groups of ten. When the bidding was over, total sales reached $2,242,900—a record for contemporary American art, and the lion's share of it for the work of Jasper Johns, notably his 1960 work *Painted Bronze* (those infamous Ballantine

Beer cans). A sea change had occurred in the world of art and art collecting; art had become a salable commodity—like a share of stock—and not everyone saw this as a positive development. Outside of Sotheby's, the Taxi Rank and File Coalition, a labor group who blasted Scull as a "parasite" who "lived off the backs of cabbies," carried signs in protest. Another group, Women in the Arts, protested that only one woman—Lee Bontecou—was represented at the auction. And the most famous remark came from Robert Rauschenberg, who was overheard saying angrily to Scull, "I've been working my ass off just for you to make that profit!" Nevertheless, the age of astronomic art prices was here to stay, ironically thanks to the work of artists whose work was aimed squarely at the middle class.

gas pumps. In Iran, the Islamic revolution in 1979 sent the Shah, the US-allied leader, into exile as student radicals under the sway of the fundamentalist Ayatollah Khomeini held fifty-two Americans hostage for 444 days.

New York City faced challenges aplenty in the 1970s. The city had descended into a morass of crime, corruption, and economic decline. Harlem, Times Square, and parts of Brooklyn and the South Bronx had reached a nadir of graffiti-covered sleaziness, ruled largely by pimps, prostitutes, drug dealers, and gangs. Muggings and rapes were on the rise, and the serial killings by the "Son of Sam" killer held Gotham in a grip of fear in the summer of 1977—the same summer that the city experienced a massive blackout that inspired rampant looting. Financial mismanagement had so crippled the city economically that it appealed to the federal government for an economic bailout and was denied. Thus the infamous headline on the October 30, 1975, edition of the *New York Daily News*: "Ford to City: Drop Dead."

Roy Lichtenstein and his new wife still frequented the galleries and museums of Manhattan, but they spent much of their time during this period in a house in the wealthy Long Island community of Southampton. Lichtenstein continued to produce work, branching out into new subject matter (mining the history of art for more ideas, bringing his unique touch to Cubism, Surrealism, Italian Futurism, and German Expressionist woodcuts) as his painting style evolved into an even more mechanical, graphic look.

a CITY BOY In THE HamPTOns

In 1970, Lichtenstein, nearing middle age and recently married, was no longer quite so suited for the bohemian Village lifestyle that had been his salvation in the late sixties—at least not full-time. In 1969, he and Dorothy had bought a carriage house on Gin Lane in the village of Southampton, a community they had come to love, and one in which the artist would spend much of the rest of his life. By 1971, the house served as both permanent residence and studio.

Southampton, said to be named after the port city of the same name in England, has a great deal of history and a longtime connection to American art. Founded in the 1640s, it includes a handful of buildings listed in the National Historic Registry that still stand today. The Thomas

Halsey House, which served as General Erskine's headquarters during the Revolutionary War, is believed to be
the first English-style house built in the state of New York.
By the middle 1800s, wealthy vacationers from the city began descending on the beaches of Southampton, establishing its reputation as a resort community for society's upper
crust. In the early 1900s, however, another type of culture
began taking root in Southampton—a growing community of artists. The great American painter William Merritt
Chase founded the Art School—today known as the Art
Village—in Shinnecock Hills in 1891, paving the way for a
host of future artists who would maintain homes and studios there, including Pollock, de Kooning, Fairfield Porter,
and Eric Fischl.

Lichtenstein first began coming to Southampton in
the late 1960s, when he and a group of friends rented a
house owned by Larry Rivers, an iconoclastic figure who
had throughout his life been a painter, a jazz musician, a
writer, and an occasional actor. Born the same year as Lichtenstein, 1923, Rivers (his birth name was Yitzroch Loiza
Grossberg) had a few other things in common with the Pop
artist. He served in the Army during World War II, and he
was very interested in jazz music. Unlike Lichtenstein, Rivers pursued music as a vocation, studying at Juilliard and
working as a jazz saxophonist before being convinced by
his wife, a painter, to try his hand at painting. He studied
art with Hans Hoffman and tackled Abstract Expressionism in his own work before becoming bored with it and
"frantic to draw the figure." Like Lichtenstein, Rivers did a
subversive version of Emanuel Leutze's *Washington Crossing
the Delaware*, and his work of the 1950s, focusing on narra-

tive paintings and portraiture, was considered, along with Johns's and Rauschenberg's work, to have prepared the stage for Pop Art. By the 1960s, Rivers was producing his own Pop-like material, his favored subject matter usually being tobacco products such as cigarettes and cigars. Rivers eventually veered more into Warhol territory, dressing flamboyantly, taking drugs, flaunting his sexual experimentation, involving himself with avant-garde theater, and befriending Beat generation writers Jack Kerouac and Allen Ginsberg. After Warhol's death in 1987, Rivers confessed to being envious of the famous artist's notoriety. Rivers died of liver cancer in 2002 in his Southampton home.

HaRD aT WORK

Lichtenstein was committed to his art, and it was difficult to pry him away from the studio. Even his first few summers in Southampton with his new wife were largely devoted to work. Lichtenstein had set up a permanent residence and studio in an old carriage house in the fabled artists' community, and although he was spending more time in the sleepy beach community on Long Island's East End, he was not by any means neglecting his painting or his growing legion of gallery-going fans. In October 1970, he completed the drawing for an enormous commissioned project—a 12-foot-by-245-foot mural to be installed on four continuous walls for the University of Düsseldorf's School of Medicine in Germany. The painting of the mural was executed by Carlene Meeker, an assistant of Lichtenstein's, and a number of the university's art students.

New York was still a few years away from being graced with one of Lichtenstein's large-scale public works, but the city's art lovers were hungry for new Lichtensteins—and one of them made history on November 18, 1970. Rudolf Zwirner, a German art dealer, purchased *Big Painting No. 6*—one of Lichtenstein's early *Brushstroke* paintings—at auction for a record price of $75,000. The purchase made Roy Lichtenstein the first living artist to have his work sold for so stratospheric a sum.

a man and his mirrors

Lichtenstein was never known for resting on his laurels, and the record-setting auction purchase of *Big Painting No. 6* did not change things. By 1971, he had moved on to his latest obsession: mirrors. The closest to pure abstraction he had come in his work for some time, the *Mirror* paintings were a radical departure from previous paintings, using Lichtenstein's trademark printer dots and rendered diagonal "streaks" to indicate light and shadow areas on a blank "glass" surface, like the line illustrations one would find in a mail-order catalog, or, indeed, a cartoon. They included no figures, furniture, or anything else "reflected" in their surfaces. The canvases themselves were shaped as ovals and circles as well as long rectangles, to add to the illusion that gallery visitors were seeing mirrors on the wall.

Lichtenstein's *Mirror* paintings, like so many of his other new ideas, were shown publicly for the first time at Leo Castelli's uptown gallery, in a show that ran from March 13 to April 3, 1971. By this point, it was difficult to predict how the critics were going to react to a new Lichtenstein series, but the *Mirrors* received a fair amount of positive response—perhaps because they represented a move from "vulgar" subject matter to more "artistic" concepts. Peter Schjeldahl reviewed the exhibition for the *New York Times*, concluding that it was "his loveliest and most prepossessing in years." Schjeldahl found the *Mirrors*, with their "splashy, mostly diagonal streaks and odd swaths suggesting a reflective surface" and distinct "graphic code" communicating a kind of depth through flatness, to be "suggestive more of Mondrian than Montgomery Ward."

THE SOHO EXODUS

The *Mirror* exhibit turned out to be the last one Lichtenstein would see in the gallery that had launched his success a decade earlier. In a move that would usher in a seismic shift in the New York art world, Castelli moved his gallery to a new building (420 West Broadway) in the downtown neighborhood south of Houston Street that had been dubbed SoHo. The 1970s would firmly establish SoHo as the new center of modern art in the city, and 420 West Broadway as the undisputed capital of avant-garde gallery space.

Castelli, who moved there in September 1971, was not alone at 420 West Broadway. The small ground-floor space was the original site of the Mary Boone Gallery, which later relocated to midtown. Boone, like Castelli, was committed to showing the work of innovative younger artists; Jean-Michel Basquiat, Julian Schnabel, Ross Bleckner, Eric Fischl, and other artists who rose to prominence in the 1980s were represented there. The gallery also held historical exhibits, showcasing groundbreaking work, including Lichtenstein's, that had influenced this new generation. John Weber, another gallery owner, also opened up shop there. And most significantly, Castelli's ex-wife, Ileana Sonnabend, fresh from her stint showing and dealing art in Europe, set up shop in the same building. Ileana and her scholarly second husband, Michael, had been largely responsible for introducing Lichtenstein and the other Pop artists to Europeans in their Paris gallery. While in Paris, the couple had discovered young European artists, such as Jannis Kounellis, Mario Merz, and Pier Paolo Calzolari, whom they were anxious to introduce to Americans. The Sonnabends established a space uptown on Madison Avenue when they returned to the United States in 1970, but it was short-lived; less than two years later, these champions of the avant-garde were drawn to the bohemian, "frontier" neighborhood of SoHo to stake their claim for the next generation of modern art.

"In a sense, SoHo in 1971 was like Paris in 1962," Alexi Worth wrote in *ArtForum*:

> Buyers were scarce. What was required was attention, excitement, talk. . . . The '70s—lean years for the art world generally—were great years for the Sonnabends. Ileana and Michael, with their unmaterialistic temperament and generosity, suited the spirit and needs of the time. In truth, they were patrons as much as dealers, supporting artists whose work echoed their intuitive avant-gardism.

Today, the Sonnabends—who maintain a residence there—are the last of these 1970s tenants to remain at 420

How SoHo Became
an Artists' Enclave

Like the Bowery, SoHo—bordered on the north by Houston Street, the east by Broadway, the west by West Broadway, and the south by Canal Street—had suffered since the end of World War II, hit especially hard by the decline of manufacturing in the city, which had gradually moved to suburban areas or overseas due to lower costs. Before it was known by the city planners' acronym, south of Houston Street was called "Hell's Hundred Acres" because of the abundance of fires that sprang up in the run-down factories and lofts.

By the 1960s, although there were still small pockets of tenants in the light manufacturing business remaining in the area, the majority of the run-down buildings were occupied by illegal squatters. Starving artists, particularly, had begun an exodus to the neighborhood lured by the dirt-cheap rents being offered by landlords desperate for any kind of rental income. Many artists entered deserted buildings illegally and refurbished them as joint workspaces and residences. These spacious, high-ceilinged structures were ideal for artists, offering ample room for large paintings, sculptures, or performance pieces. Unfortunately, the squatters' presence in these buildings was in violation of fire codes and other regulations, so the artists often had to go to elaborate extremes to avoid being discovered, like hiding kitchens and beds in case of a fire inspector's visit.

For a time, the city's Buildings Department fought against vagabond artists taking over the abandoned space, until a significant change occurred in 1971. The one most responsible for the change was George Maciunas, a pioneer of the Fluxus movement, a school of art influenced by avant-garde music that was widely seen as a forerunner of, and an influence on, Pop Art in the early 1960s. Maciunas, who had become an outspoken proponent of artists' rights, attained the financial aid of a forward-thinking foundation called the Kaplan Fund, which began to turn the tide. Kaplan offered $100,000 for Maciunas's bold renewal project, which involved converting many of SoHo's deserted cast-iron buildings into low-cost housing specifically aimed at the artistic community. Although these new co-ops—available for minimal down payments—were still technically illegal, Maciunas was successful in communicating his ambition to the public and the press—namely, to prevent artists from leaving the already economically depressed city in droves. A group called the SoHo Artists Association joined in the fight, openly daring the city to scuttle the project and toss them all out.

Amazingly, perhaps due to the overwhelmingly pro-artist sentiment whipped up by a sympathetic press, the city not only gave in, but also sweetened the situation. In January 1971, Donald Elliott, the city's planning chief, decreed SoHo essentially an artists-only enclave: to legally live or work inside the forty-three-square-block area, an artist had to obtain a document called an "Artist's Certification" from the city's Department of Cultural Affairs proving that he or she was a working artist. These restrictions proved to be very loose: art collectors, art dealers, even artists' spouses who had such nonartistic vocations as banking or stock speculation managed to obtain the desired certifications. Although the "JLWQA" (Joint Living Working Quarters for Artists) model—endorsed by New York City Mayor John Lindsay and the state's art-collector governor, Nelson Rockefeller—certainly benefited struggling artists, its larger aim was to give a shot in the arm to New York's decaying inner city. Today's SoHo—the one of sky-high rents and luxury retailers, where legitimately starving artists are rarely seen—is a direct result of the flow of money and influence into the formerly decrepit area in the 1970s and 1980s.

West Broadway, the rest having moved to other Manhattan neighborhoods, and many to Chelsea, which has since become another modern art outpost.

STUDIES AND SOURCES AT SVA

While the heart of New York's modern art was shifting downtown, the city itself was still serving Roy Lichtenstein as an incubator of new ideas. As the metal subway signs had begotten Lichtenstein's enameled steel sculptures in 1964, the classical friezes on the entablatures atop New York's grand old buildings inspired a series of large, finished drawings in the 1970s. The *Entablatures* series, with its representations of architectural relief and abstract motifs, provided an opportunity to experiment with spatial illusion, and the play of light and shadow. By reversing the figure-ground relationship, Lichtenstein eliminated outline entirely in the drawings; all the line work represents shadows cast by an unseen light source. He used the technique in 1964 in *Temple of Apollo*, another piece, like the *Entablatures*, where he translated a photographic source into an illustrative picture distinctly his own. The *Entablatures* series can be divided into two distinct series: the black-and-white paintings executed between 1971 and 1972, and the full-color ones done from 1974 through 1976.

The great majority of Lichtenstein's paintings, however, still started as drawings. November of 1971 saw the first exhibition of Lichtenstein's drawings—mostly studies for his comic strips, temples, and modular paintings—at one of New York City's proudest institutions of artistic training, the School of Visual Arts, or SVA (209 E. 23rd Street between 2nd and 3rd) in the area known as Gramercy.

The largest independent undergraduate art college in the United States, SVA traces its existence back to the Manhattan Academy of Newspaper Art, established in the 1940s as an illustration school for returning World War II veterans. Its founder was one of America's most legendary icons of cartooning, illustration, and art education, Burne Hogarth, who came to New York from Chicago at a young age and found steady employment in newspaper illustration, cartooning, and editing. In 1936, he was handed the assignment that would define his career: the *Tarzan* newspaper strip, which he drew for twelve years, in the process pioneering a new standard of sequential storytelling that influenced future generations of comic book and comic strip artists.

Already an experienced teacher, Hogarth joined with financier Silas H. Rhodes in 1947 to mold his Newspaper School into the Cartoonists and Illustrators School. After years of steady growth, it was renamed the School of Visual Arts in 1956. SVA's students and instructors have included many of the world's most renowned comics illustrators, including Wally Wood, Al Williamson, Joe Orlando, Carmine Infantino, Klaus Janson, and Walter Simonson. The school has also produced leaders in the fields of design and film and several notable figures in the world of fine art who took New York by storm in the late 1970s and 1980s—Keith Haring, Kenny Scharf, and Jean-Michel Basquiat, inheritors of the Pop artists' avant-garde mantle.

The drawings shown at SVA in 1971 gave Lichtenstein's fans a glimpse of his unique artistic processes; a series that he began in late 1973 brought viewers right into his studio—albeit a two-dimensional version of it. If the *Entablatures*, with their distinctly impersonal, decorative subject matter, appeared to put to rest the notion that Lichtenstein was becoming more introspective and self-referential, his *Artist's Studio* series seemed to suggest otherwise.

OLD MASTERS AND NEW TECHNIQUES

The *Artist's Studio* series, which included five paintings executed between 1973 and 1974, was another step away from "low art" and simple compositions and toward more complex subject matter. It was also another exploration into the overriding theme of art about art. The seed for these works was a number of slick reproductions of Matisse's paintings that Lichtenstein had come across in books. Noting that the Impressionist master had incorporated his earlier work in paintings such as *The Red Studio* and *The Pink Studio* (both 1911), with their depictions of art in various media in a studio setting, Lichtenstein couldn't resist revisiting the theme. In keeping with his modus operandi, his first *Artist's Studio* painting (and some others late in the series) directly appropriated imagery from Matisse, but in many of the subsequent canvases, the only artist whose work Lichtenstein cribbed from in his studio interiors was Lichtenstein himself.

In *Artists' Studio: Look*, *Mickey* (1973), Lichtenstein's epochal image of Disney characters hangs on the wall over a couch. The Matisse influence is evident in the philodendron in a vase next to the couch, its leaves poking into the plane of the word-balloon-dominated painting on the wall. Lichtenstein's growing repertoire of visual elements is also on display, notably the distinctive mirror on the right wall and the entablature-like pattern near the ceiling. *Artist's Studio: Foot Medication* demonstrates the diagonal lines that Lichtenstein had started using to indicate shadow—an alternative to his use of Ben-Day dots.

a new spin on still life

Lichtenstein was looking increasingly to the past for inspiration. In 1972, and continuing through 1976 with the *Still Life* series, he began dabbling in a medium that he had rarely explored before. His growing use of pictorial references to other artistic genres is apparent in *Things on the Wall* (1973). The composition references the work of William Harnett and John Frederick Peto in its layering of disparate images. Lichtenstein establishes a wooden armature, defined by a shading and texture technique—a Cubist-style "faux bois" wood grain—that is a departure from the customary Ben-Day dot style. The wood-grain technique is a stylistic nod to another age-old painting style established in the nineteenth century called "trompe l'oeil" (literally, "trick of the eye" in French). Lichtenstein so enjoyed using the technique—manipulating the thickness of the lines and the color of the "wood"—that he began experimenting with other textural tricks in his 1970s and 1980s paintings.

Cubist Still Life from 1974 continues Lichtenstein's homage to Picasso, using Picasso's recognizable device of a guitar in the composition, as well as the wood-grain technique. Lichtenstein was so enamored of his experiments in Cubism that he spent the better part of the 1970s exploring other "-isms": Futurism, Purism, and a distinctly German variant of Expressionism.

GOING NATIVE: THE AMERICAN INDIAN SERIES

The art styles that Lichtenstein explored in the 1970s were many and varied, and he didn't stop with American and European schools of painting. Downtown from the galleries of SoHo, in New York's bustling financial district, is an art museum that would not readily spring to mind when one thinks of Roy Lichtenstein, but the art collection inside nevertheless had an impact on his 1970s work. The National Museum of the American Indian (1 Bowling Green), at the southern tip of Broadway across from Battery Park, was founded by the Smithsonian Institution and is also known as the George Gustav Heye Center, named for the New York banker who amassed the 800,000-piece collection of Indian artifacts that forms the foundation of the museum's collection. The walls of the interior elliptical rotunda feature painted murals by Lichtenstein's old drawing teacher, Reginald Marsh.

Lichtenstein first encountered the Heye collection in the 1960s or 1970s, thanks to another friend who was an avid collector of Native American arts and crafts. Jonathan Holstein, a writer and art dealer, met and befriended Lichtenstein and other contemporary artists while working as a photographer in the 1960s. Holstein shared with Roy and Dorothy his passion for paintings, quilts, and other items in the Heye collection. These objects would be the impetus for Lichtenstein's *Amerindian* series of paintings, executed between 1979 and 1981, as was the work of George Catlin, an early American painter who traveled among the tribal peoples during the 1830s and captured them in his images of the American West. Lichtenstein considered Catlin's work reminiscent of the paintings of Remington, the most famous chronicler of the Old West on canvas. If this was all not enough inspiration, the Lichtensteins' home in Southampton was near a Shinnecock Indian reservation, and the couple took a rapt interest in their neighbors, attending pow-wows at the reservation.

mILESTONE aT THE WHITNEY

By the summer of 1978, Lichtenstein had the perfect showcase for his 1970s paintings referencing the work of other artists—the aptly named *Art About Art* exhibition at the Whitney Museum of American Art (now located at 99 Gansevoort Street) from July 19 through September 24.

Art About Art consisted of around one hundred objects—paintings, sculptures, prints, collages, drawings, and a smattering of photo and video art—drawn from the previous twenty-five years. The "Popists" and their influences were well represented: Warhol, Johns, Samaras, Indiana, Oldenburg, Wesselman, Segal, Rauschenberg, Larry Rivers, Joseph Cornell, Peter Saul, and Malcolm Morley all had work in the show, in addition to several pieces by Lichtenstein. The exhibit was divided into three areas of study: "About the Artist," concentrating on depictions of brushes, brushstrokes, paint tubes, and canvases; "About Old Masters," collecting homages to and parodies of work by the likes of Rembrandt, daVinci, and Velázquez; and "About Modern Masters," with images of more recent giants, such as Picasso, Matisse, and Mondrian.

While lamenting the absence of European artists from the collection (the Whitney exhibits only the work of American artists), Hilton Kramer singled out Lichtenstein in his review for the *New York Times* as the artist most representative of the show's theme: "Mr. Lichtenstein quite dominates whole sections of the show," he wrote. "He has also designed the cover of the book and the poster for the show. In some ways the most systematic of the artists

The Deconstructionist

Lichtenstein's legacy remains a subject of controversy in some circles, largely due to the efforts of a Hartford Art School student who started, in 1979, what would become a career-defining project that continues to this day. David Barsalou, a comic book collector, art history buff, and regular attendee of comic conventions throughout the 1970s, wrote a term paper for an art history class on the origins of Lichtenstein's comic book paintings, as well as several similarly themed works by Warhol and Mel Ramos. Encouraged by his professor and mentor Jack Goldstein, Barsalou expanded his search, focusing on Lichtenstein, by far the most prolific purveyor of the style.

In those pre-eBay, pre-Internet days, Barsalou's task was a challenging one, although his own extensive collection of Golden Age and Silver Age comic books, original art (including the William Overgard illustration that spawned *I Can See the Whole Room*), and other collectibles, which he had been accumulating since 1961, provided a strong foundation. The results of this decades-long artistic scavenger hunt are on display in "Deconstructing Roy Lichtenstein," an online gallery hosted on the website Flickr, in which Barsalou matches up Lichtenstein works with their original comic book sources or probable sources. Much of the attribution of Lichtenstein's sources in this book (and in some instances, speculation on them) has been researched or confirmed using this online resource, which contains more than 1,200 (and counting) images.

As one might expect, Barsalou's project, which first

went online in 1999, several years after Lichtenstein's death, has not been positively received by the Roy Lichtenstein Foundation, which tightly controls the use of Lichtenstein art and has resisted some critics' characterization of the artist as a plagiarist who has benefited financially from the work of other, lesser known and less well compensated artists. The foundation has gone on record to defend against such accusations, in at least one case using language that seems to question whether the original comics artists were even "artists" at all.

"Roy's work was a wonderment of the graphic formulae and the codification of sentiment that had been worked out by others," Jack Cowart, chairman of the foundation, said in a 2006 interview with the *Boston Globe*. "Barsalou's thesis notwithstanding, the panels were changed in scale, color, treatment, and in their implications. There is no exact copy." Cowart continued, "This wasn't supposed to be about exploiting the exploited. We are all in favor of having the *drawers* [emphasis mine] and writers receive as much credit as humanly possible. We owe them esteem but can't pay them back for the royalties they might have received."

"It is important to recognize the original artists as 'Real American Artists,' many of them just as educated as [Lichtenstein]," insisted Barsalou, expressing infuriation over such dismissals of the comics illustrators' talents:

Just because they chose a different path . . . doesn't make them any less an artist. I've always hated that separation. To Hell with all the Artspeak theory and diatribe; art is art as far as I'm concerned. Like jazz and blues, comic books are a true American art form. It's important to emphasize that comic book artists created the original imagery Lichtenstein copied. Yes, comics were already art. . . . Go figure.

However, the statute of limitations for copyright infringement on all these images is long expired—a fact that has no bearing on Barsalou's decision to continue his exhaustive search for Lichtenstein source material and his determination to award a generation of comic book artists with the acknowledgment and respect that has largely eluded them in the "serious" art world.

who produce art about art, he seems to be making his way through a version of every major oeuvre of the modern period."

a PLace among THe GReaTS

As the decade came to a close, Lichtenstein was prepared to take his place among the greats of American art. On May 23, 1979, he was presented with a distinguished honor—induction into the American Academy of Arts and Letters—in a ceremony in New York. Among the other thirteen inductees were Lichtenstein's friend and Southampton neighbor Larry Rivers; painter Joan Mitchell; architect John M. Johansen; sculptor Tony Smith; a trio of poets, Joseph Brodsky, Robert Hayden, and John Hollander; composer Ned Rorem; and essayist and novelist Susan Sontag (who made her own possibly unintentional contribution to the Pop movement with her 1964 essay "Notes on Camp," which brought the concept of camp into the mainstream cultural consciousness). Thus, a few years shy of his sixtieth birthday, the mild-mannered former Rutgers art professor with the self-deprecating wit and relentless work ethic who found his true voice in his late thirties officially joined the pantheon of American artists who mattered. Still, much of Lichtenstein's largest, most ambitious work was still ahead of him—and the city of his birth would be the main beneficiary.

Pop's Progeny

In the same way that Pop Art was a reaction to Abstract Expressionism, its modern offshoot style, known as Post-Pop or neo-Pop, was a reaction to the Minimalism and Conceptualism that had dominated the 1970s. Among the young pioneers that made up this movement, a few could be described as heirs to Lichtenstein's Image Duplicator throne.

Haim Steinbach was an Israeli-born American citizen who studied art at Pratt Institute in Brooklyn. Active in the East Village art scene in the late 1970s and the 1980s, Steinbach was influenced by Surrealism, Cézanne, and Marcel Duchamp. Although his appropriation of consumer items in his large works echoed Lichtenstein and Warhol, Steinbach's work—often composed of shelf arrangements of found objects from flea markets and other sources—is more evocative of Rauschenberg's combines and Duchamp's ready-mades.

Sherrie Levine, a photographer and conceptual artist educated at the University of Wisconsin, took Lichtenstein's philosophy to the next extreme: a member of the school known as "Appropriationists," along with Cindy Sherman, David Salle, and Robert Longo, Levine courted controversy by photographing reproductions of other artists' work and showing the photos as original works. In 1990, she included Lichtenstein's own comic strip paintings and prints in a piece called *Collage/Cartoon*.

The artist most readily regarded as Lichtenstein's heir apparent is undoubtedly Jeff Koons. Born in York,

Pennsylvania, and educated at art colleges in Maryland and Chicago, Koons worked as a Wall Street commodities trader before embarking on a professional art career in 1980. He set up a Factory-like studio operation in a SoHo loft and employed more than thirty people to assist him in producing work.

Koons is well known for his elevation of kitsch subject matter into sculpture, such as *Balloon Dog* (1994–2000)—a 10-foot-tall metal depiction of a toy dog constructed with balloons, painted bright red for stunning visual effect. Koons is an admirer of Lichtenstein's sculptural works. The younger artist, commenting on the visual effect of Lichtenstein's *Untitled II*, the *Brushstroke* sculpture installed at New York's Seagram Building, said:

> Moving paint around in an expressionist way is only one form of gesture. One has to make an action in order to bring forth a work of art, but it may be a matter of producing an idea, not a physical act. I've thought about the question of gestures a great deal in the last few years, and I believe that the act of making art is itself a gesture—a gesture in the mind. Roy's work has helped me understand that.

All the Neo-Popists have been subject to harsh criticism and, in some cases, lawsuits over the originality of their appropriated images. But the success they have attained and continue to attain proves that the spirit of Pop Art —in all its infuriating, controversial glory— lives on in one form or another.

8

a new YORK Legacy

THE ARTIST MARKS HIS CITY

The 1980s in America started with a struggling economy and ended with the country on the cusp of its first war in Iraq. The Cold War with the Soviet Union, which had dominated both nations since the end of World War II, came to a dramatic end in 1989 with the fall of the Berlin Wall in Germany, leaving the United States—as it had been in the late 1940s—the world's only true superpower. Under the presidency of Ronald Reagan, and that of his vice president and successor, George H.W. Bush, the US economy soared, bringing a new era of materialism. Arkansas governor Bill Clinton was elected in 1992 after an economic downturn in the wake of the conflict in the Middle East soured voters on Bush. In the 1990s, once again, the nation's economy boomed, as the rise of the Internet inspired a new generation of savvy entrepreneurs and investors. The "new media" economy ensured that Clinton's popularity survived even as a presidential sex scandal with a White House intern led to his impeachment. The dot-com bubble would burst toward the end of the decade, but not before the technological advances of the 1990s' "information age" had irrevocably changed society.

Wall Street was booming by the mid-1980s, bringing not only a revitalized economy to New York City, but a level of conspicuous consumption that had not been seen since the Pop-inspiring days of the 1950s. However, homelessness, crime, and racial tension remained major problems in the city, plaguing both Mayor Ed Koch and his successor, David Dinkins. Violence in the Queens neighborhood of Howard Beach and the Bensonhurst section of Brooklyn made national news, along with the case of "subway vigilante" Bernhard Goetz. Unemployment and crime rose again in the early 1990s, and voters rejected Dinkins's bid for reelection in favor of a no-nonsense former prosecutor, Rudolph Giuliani. The 1990s saw both an economic boom and a social renaissance of sorts for New York City, with crime and joblessness dipping to their lowest levels in decades. Although Giuliani's reign was also marked by some controversial events, usually involving issues of racial bias by the police, the law-and-order mayor is largely credited with cleaning up New York City and helping restore it to the top of American cities as the new millennium dawned.

Art continued to thrive throughout the 1980s and 1990s, as new stars such as Haring, Basquiat, Schnabel, Koons, and others reached their prime, and the art auction market remained hot. But the art world also took some hits: Andy Warhol died of complications from a gall bladder operation on February 22, 1987, and his friends and protégés, Haring and Basquiat, would also not see the dawn of the 1990s. With Warhol's passing, Roy Lichtenstein became Pop's major living master; his new work was still a common sight in Leo Castelli's galleries, though the majority of his time and effort by this point in his life was spent creating large public works that would cement his legacy in the city of his birth.

THE DISAPPEARING MURAL OF GREENE STREET

Business was good for Leo Castelli as the 1980s dawned—good enough for the veteran art dealer to open up an annex to his existing space—the Greene Street Gallery in Greenwich Village (142 Greene Street). And what better way to celebrate the opening of the new gallery space than with a truly major painting by Roy Lichtenstein, one of Castelli's most renowned artistic discoveries?

The so-called Greene Street Mural, painted in early December 1983 and on view to the public until the middle of January 1984, was Lichtenstein's most ambitious attempt yet to create a retrospective of his own artwork by using a collage of familiar motifs. The huge wall painting, which Lichtenstein executed with the help of assistants, occupied the entire north wall of the gallery, spanning almost 96 feet in length and reaching 18 feet high. The artist conceived the mural as a series of rectangles that spectators could walk by and in which they'd recognize the objects and themes that had come to define Lichtenstein's body of work. Bernice

Rose, the curator of the 1987 Museum of Modern Art exhibit *The Drawings of Roy Lichtenstein* described the effect of the Greene Street Mural:

> The spectator traverses each rectangle in turn, walking past a retrospective of themes from Lichtenstein's work, expanded to giant size, as if seen by a little child in a giant toy shop. The notion. . . . that the painting is a world—bigger than life, but flat and, like the world through the looking glass, virtually impenetrable—is even more pronounced.

Indeed, one can find a plethora of by-now-familiar Lichtensteinian elements among the panels of the finished mural: a Surrealist nude figure with red-dot shading; Venetian blinds opening to reveal a Picasso-esque head; Art Deco patterns; numerous areas of shading depicted with dots and diagonal lines; pyramids; mirrors; and cartoon illustrations of what appear to be a bathroom tissue roll and a closed toilet, perhaps hearkening back to his early paintings of household appliances and interiors.

The truly interesting point to make about the Greene Street Mural—the one that says the most about Lichtenstein's attitude toward art—is the limited time it was available for public view before it was purposely painted over. The only Lichtenstein mural proposed by the artist himself rather than commissioned by a patron was designed to not last—to be seen and then to disappear; to be the object of an exhibition without itself being a salable object. Discussing the concept behind the mural with a reporter, Dorothy Lichtenstein said, "There was all this conceptual art around—so Roy wanted to do this as an impermanent piece of work that would be the exhibition but not an object. His work was becoming very costly, and he loved the idea of doing something that couldn't be sold—just erased." Photographer Bob Adelman posed a question to Lichtenstein: Why invest so much toil and effort into a project that was destined to fade away? The artist answered, "For the pleasure of the dance."

However, such a trailblazing work was destined not to fade entirely into obscurity: More than thirty years later, a new generation of art aficionados had a chance to experience Lichtenstein's Greene Street Mural, or at least the closest modern approximation of it. In 2015, the Gagosian Gallery presented *Roy Lichtenstein: Greene Street Mural*, a full-scale painted replica of the original work, based on documentation from Lichtenstein's studio and produced under the supervision of one of his former studio assistants. In keeping with the ephemeral spirit of the original, the replica was destroyed at the close of the exhibition.

Leo Castelli's tenure at the Greene Street address proved to be limited as well. By 1990, Castelli had again moved his operations uptown, leaving both SoHo locations for a new site at 59 East 79th Street. (In 1990, the Pace Wildenstein gallery took over 142 Greene Street, opening up a new exhibition space for its expanding roster of artists.)

InnovaTinG in THE EIGHTIES

The Greene Street Mural was Lichtenstein's major project of the early 1980s, but it was far from his only one. On the heels of his induction into the American Academy of Arts and Sciences in 1979, in May 1980 he was awarded an honorary doctorate of fine arts from Southampton College, where he had begun to teach courses after he and Dorothy had settled on Long Island. Truly an elder statesman of art as he approached his twilight years, Lichtenstein had come full circle in his own work, influencing the younger artistic generation that was making its mark in the early 1980s. The Pop-influenced works of Scharf, Basquiat, and Haring had begun to acquire buzz in the art world, and by 1981, up-and-coming artists such as Jeff Koons, Sherrie Levine, and Haim Steinbach were making a practice of doing what Lichtenstein had been doing, often to great indignation and ridicule, since the 1960s—appropriating the art of others as the basis for their own work. The concept of art about art, it seemed, had finally come of age.

While Lichtenstein was encouraging to the new guard in the New York art world, he was nowhere near ready for retirement himself. He continued to experiment with new motifs and ideas and to put interesting new spins on some of his old ones. In 1981, he even took a crack at the style he had long ago abandoned in favor of cartoon characters: Abstract Expressionism. He executed four *Woman* paintings, based on the famous series done by Willem de Kooning in the late 1950s.

He explored the artist's studio process in a different way with his *Paintings* and *Two Paintings* series in 1982. *Silver Frame* (1984) juxtaposes actual Abstract Expressionist brushstrokes with Lichtenstein's 2-D Pop brushstrokes, inside an illustratively rendered "frame" border. *Two Paintings: Dagwood* (1983) takes the concept on step further: One side of the composition is a classic cartoon image, Dagwood from the *Blondie* comic strip; the other is an abstract collage of brushstrokes. A "frame" element separates the images. It was as if Lichtenstein (who claimed he loved many of the Abstract Expressionists) was finally acknowledging the relative merits of each school of art.

Lichtenstein's work had also found more interest outside New York. From May to June of 1981, the Saint Louis Art Museum presented a large exhibition of the artist's paintings and sculptures, curated by Dr. Jack Cowart, later the chairman of the Roy Lichtenstein Foundation. In 1983, Lichtenstein's *Brushstrokes in Flight* was purchased for the ground-floor entrance of the airport in Columbus, Ohio— a fitting tribute from the state where the New York native spent his formative years as a teacher and a working artist.

HISTORY IN THE HAMPTONS

Ivan Karp may never have changed his negative opinion of *Look, Mickey*—the painting that made its public debut at Lichtenstein's historic first Castelli Gallery exhibit—but by 1982 there was no denying its importance in the history of American modern art. On August 8 of that year, *Look, Mickey* was featured with several other pieces (including other "hidden" early work, *Popeye* and *Wimpy [Tweet]*), both from 1961, in an exhibit at the Parrish Art Museum in Southampton.

The museum displays a wealth of American art, with a special emphasis on artists who have made Long Island's East End their home. The Impressionist works of William Merritt Chase and realist works of Fairfield Porter are well represented, and pieces by Southampton notables such as Pollock, de Kooning, Lee Krasner, Dan Flavin, John Chamberlain, Chuck Close, and April Gornik make up a substantial part of the collection. The Parrish today owns one piece by Lichtenstein: *Apple with Brushstrokes* (1984), a collage of printed and painted paper mounted on board. Dorothy Lichtenstein would go on to serve as a trustee for the museum.

a TOWERING achievement

Although Roy and Dorothy loved Southampton, the siren call of Manhattan was again too much for Roy to resist for long, and in 1984 he returned to the Big Apple part-time to live and work, this time setting up shop in a loft, a spacious, brightly lit space with wood floors and exposed piping (105 East 29th Street). Displaying his workmanlike, disciplined approach, Lichtenstein outfitted the studio with six specially designed easels that rotated from top to bottom to show paintings in progress at various angles. Another quirky personal touch the artist added was a huge painting of Swiss cheese, which covered the door of the freight elevator. It was a suitable base to work, as Lichtenstein's next big project, which required a great deal of time in the city, was coming down the pike later that year.

The Greene Street Mural was long gone by autumn of 1984, but it was surely in Lichtenstein's mind as he sat down to tackle the challenge presented to him in his latest, biggest commissioned work: *Mural with Blue Brushstroke*, a two-story magnum opus for the lobby of what is today called the AXA Equitable Center (787 Seventh Avenue). The art consultants for Equitable Insurance had seen Lichtenstein's mural at Castelli's gallery in 1983, and promptly decided they wanted a picture of that scope for their new office building, knowing, at first, nothing but the dimensions the work had to fill: a daunting 68 feet high by 32 feet wide.

Equitable, in 1984 already headquartered in the largest office building in America occupied by a single company, had big plans for its towering new home, which would open in 1986. The limestone-and-granite building was intended to be an eye-catching attraction for visitors, featuring several pieces of public art, with Lichtenstein's mural as the breathtaking centerpiece. In contrast to Lichtenstein's ironic collage of images, the other large mural in the lobby at the time was Thomas Hart Benton's multipanel 1930s masterpiece *America Today*, depicting, as indicated on its label, "the economic and social life of the nation on the eve of the Depression." Admiring the theme of Benton's work, Lichtenstein set out to create the opposite: a work with no theme at all. "Benton has a definite social point of view," he told an interviewer. "I have an ambivalent point of view, which I'm getting across. I can't make out the world and it shows."

Photographer Bob Adelman chronicled Lichtenstein's work in progress for the mural, noting the atmosphere of the studio—tidy, spacious, and often with classical music playing in the background—while the artist and two of his assistants, James DePasquale and Rob McKeever, worked on the large maquette for the mural. Lichtenstein saw murals as having an architectural structure, and painstakingly studied the building plans to determine how the image could be incorporated within the structure of the building. He chose a number of elements, most of which echoed one theme or another that he had toyed with in his art for the past twenty-five years.

After Lichtenstein finished the maquette—a long and involved process of choosing, refining, deleting, and juxtaposing elements—work began on the full-size mural. Lichtenstein and his assistants took nearly six weeks to complete the project. The result is one of the largest public art works in the city, five stories high, dominating the atrium lobby of the Equitable Center, and catching the eye of midtown passersby. In contrast to the disposable nature of its predecessor at the Greene Street Gallery, the finished work, *Mural with Blue Brushstroke*, is, in the words of Calvin Tompkins, "an indelible sight, a permanent monument (as permanent as anything gets in New York) to Pop Art."

In the massive multicolored, multitextured expanse of *Mural with Blue Brushstroke*, observers will find numerous examples of the artist paying homage to both other artists and to his own eclectic body of work. There is a figure in the upper left holding a beach ball, an amalgam of a figure from Léger's *The Dance* and Lichtenstein's own

Girl with Ball. The ball doubles as a cartoonish sun throwing off rays, a reference to Lichtenstein's landscapes from the 1960s. The door and window blind in the bottom left and upper right, respectively, could refer to works from Lichtenstein's *Studio* or *Interiors* paintings. The door also comes from *Knock Knock*, a 1961 black-and-white painting that depicts comic book sound effects imposed over a two-dimensional door. (The actual words "Knock Knock," intended as part of the composition, were the only major element nixed by the artist's clients at Equitable, for reasons unclear). The flagstone element near the middle right edge is taken from Jasper Johns; above it, the Swiss-cheese area calls to mind the work of Jean Arp. There is a decorative Lichtenstein entablature separating the top of the composition from the bottom, and a Greek column, reminiscent of his temple paintings, framing the upper right edge. The triangle and French curve bring to mind both Lichtenstein's 1970s *Still Lifes* and the work of Frank Stella. And there is the large blue brushstroke that slices through the middle of the collage, the dominant element after which the mural is named. Perhaps the element that truly makes the most pertinent visual statement about the mural and its location is the illustrative hand with sponge, apparently wiping the flat surface of the image. The effect is that all the elements beneath the hand are two-dimensional, and wiping them away would simply clear the surface of the building's window.

Approximately thirty gallons of paint were used in *Mural with Blue Brushstroke*, and Lichtenstein's palette included eighteen distinct colors—substantially more than he had used in previous paintings.

Reaction to the sweeping work was largely positive, with the *New York Times* calling it "an event of major artistic importance . . . mark[ing] a commitment to art on the part of a prominent American corporation that is as generous and innovative as any before."

QUESTIONING PERFECTION

In the mid- to late 1980s, Lichtenstein took his interest in composition—and in applying scientific principles to art— in a different, irreverent direction with his *Perfect/Imperfect* paintings. This series consists of geometric abstractions— triangles, spheres, and other shapes—in deliberately garish arrangements. Their purpose, Lichtenstein said, was to parody the generic framed artwork that hangs on the walls of television sitcoms. What was the difference, then, between *Perfect* and *Imperfect*? Simply, the *Perfect* paintings neatly fit in the rectangular confines of the canvas, while the elements in the *Imperfect* paintings do not, protruding beyond the imaginary borders of the frame. "It's supposed to be humorous," Lichtenstein said of the series. "Art becomes this game of whether I hit the edges."

Whether or not the *Perfect* and *Imperfect* paintings deserved their tongue-in-cheek name, the Museum of Modern Art—where the Pop Art movement was officially christened in 1963—was the perfect venue to mount the first major retrospective of Roy Lichtenstein's drawings in 1987. Curated by Bernice Rose, it was the first such show the museum had ever organized for a living artist.

The museum, known affectionately to New Yorkers as MOMA, is one of the world's preeminent centers of contemporary art and the leading source of research material on modern art worldwide.

Of all the museums in New York City, the MOMA boasts the most Roy Lichtenstein works in its collection, including two of the most important early Pop paintings, *Girl with Ball* (1961) and *Drowning Girl* (1963); the 1960s landscape painting *Seascape with Dunes* (1965); *Artist's Studio: The Dance* (1974) from the *Artist's Studio* series; a 1976 *Entablature*; and a number of drawings and sketches, including studies for *Brushstrokes*, the 1980s *Imperfect* paintings, and *Artist's Studio: The Dance*.

The retrospective of Lichtenstein's drawings went on the road after closing at the MOMA on June 2, 1987, traveling to museums across the United States and Europe.

CENTRAL PARK'S SCULPTURE GARDEN

By summer 1988, Lichtenstein was splitting his time between Southampton and a studio/residence in Greenwich Village (745 Washington Street) in a former iron foundry built in 1912—a fitting domicile for an artist so drawn to both the past and the industrial process. He resurrected his 1960s comic strip motifs in his work of that year, specifically in his *Reflections* series (where he applied his mirror stylings to the images). He continued his explorations of purely abstract design in his *Plus and Minus* paintings, channeling the spirit of that master of simple geometric abstraction, Piet Mondrian.

Lichtenstein was also creating three-dimensional abstractions in 1988. In one, he took his *Brushstrokes* idea and applied it to a huge public sculpture. *Brushstroke*, a 30-foot-high painted aluminum sculpture that Lichtenstein fashioned in 1987, was installed at the Doris C. Freedman Plaza, the scenic entrance to New York's Central Park at 5th Avenue and 60th Street, north of Grand Army Plaza.

The plaza is named for Doris Chanin Freedman (1928–81), a longtime patron and advocate of the arts who served as the first director of the New York City Department of Cultural Affairs and the president of City Walls. Freedman merged City Walls with the Public Arts Council in 1977 to create the city's Public Art Fund, which for twenty-five years organized rotating six-month sculpture exhibits at the plaza. A popular gathering spot for outdoor brown-bag lunches for workers in the southern Central Park area, the sculptures add an element of fun, fascination, and whimsy to the plaza, drawing gazes and snapshots like the horse-drawn carriages and portrait artists that commonly frequent the area.

The *Brushstroke* sculpture at Central Park (now in the hands of a private collector) was a fixture for New Yorkers and tourists until May 1989, but its creator was far less stationary that year, traveling extensively to execute more large public works of art. For two months (March 15 through May 15), Lichtenstein was artist-in-residence at the American Academy in Rome. After that, he traveled to

Tel Aviv, Israel, where he worked on a 23-by-54-foot mural for the entrance hall of the Tel Aviv Museum of Art. And in the summer, he began work on *Bauhaus Stairway: The Large Version*, a mural for the new headquarters of the Creative Artists Agency (designed by architect I. M. Pei) in Beverly Hills. And as if anyone needed further proof that Lichtenstein had attained a stature in the art world that his 1950s and 1960s critics could never have fathomed, November 7, 1989, put him in the record books again. The sale of *Torpedo . . . Los!*, one of Lichtenstein's most famous war comic paintings, for $5.5 million at a Christie's auction placed him in the upper echelon of living American artists. Only de Kooning and Johns had ever commanded such prices for their work.

Lichtenstein began experimenting with a new technique in his *Interiors* paintings, beginning in 1990: painting with sponges. The *Interiors* were inspired in part by furniture advertisements in telephone books; they depicted banal domestic environments of modern-day living. *Interior with Mirrored Wall* (1991), a part of the Guggenheim's collection, provides an example. Lichtenstein was still fascinated with two-dimensional representations of glass reflections and of light and shadow on surfaces, as demonstrated by the mirrored wall and the polished dark surface of the grand piano, cropped at the lower left corner. References to art—both his own and others'—are evident: the framed pictures on the wall are Lichtenstein's, and the decorative pattern on the floor covering is a reference to Henri Matisse.

a Head for modern sculpture

From October 7, 1990, through January 15, 1991, Lichtenstein's fans, young and old, were treated to a rare sight, while his detractors were given a fresh round of ammunition. A MOMA exhibition featured the artist's comic strip paintings side by side with the source material that inspired them—in many cases, for the very first time. The *High and Low: Modern Art and Popular Culture* exhibition featured examples of twentieth-century art alongside sources and other ephemera. It was a fascinating look at recent art history and its symbiotic relationship with popular culture. Lichtenstein's own concerns, however, were firmly planted in the present. Two of his *Interiors* paintings were shown in the Whitney Museum's prestigious *Biennial Exhibition* in spring 1991. Meanwhile, he was also working on a major public piece.

In 1974, Lichtenstein had traveled to the Lippincott foundry in Connecticut to fashion the pieces of a 30-foot-high sculpture of metal, wood, and polyurethane called *Modern Head*. The sculpture was assembled at its destination, Santa Anita Fashion Park in Arcadia, California, where it remained until 1988. In 1991, Lichtenstein was commissioned to create another *Modern Head* for New York, this one to be displayed as public art in Battery Park City, in Lower Manhattan near the downtown Financial District.

The 1991 *Modern Head* is two feet taller than the original and constructed of gleaming steel. Like the *Brushstroke* sculpture at Doris C. Freedman Plaza, its installation in

Battery Park City was organized by the Public Art Fund. *Modern Head,* which remained on display until October 31, 1991, was described by *New York Times* art critic Michael Brenson as "Mr. Lichtenstein's Nike of Samothrace . . . high-spirited, down to earth, and popular in imagery, but at the same time detached, rigorously unsentimental and increasingly abstract the more you consider its presence."

In 1992, Lichtenstein revisited the sculptural head theme again, this time incorporating it with a tribute to another great artist. *Barcelona Head* is a massive, 64-foot-high sculpture constructed of multiple colored ceramic tiles, constructed to be placed in Barcelona, on the site of the former naval yard where Christopher Columbus had once docked his ships. The inspiration for the work was legendary Catalan architect Antoni Gaudí (1852–1926), who blended Gothic and Art Nouveau sensibilities in his unique, avant-garde buildings, such as Barcelona's own Park Guell, Casa Batlló, and the famous Sagrada Familia Temple, the city's most visited attraction. The project was commissioned for the 1992 Summer Olympics in Barcelona—another feather in the cap of the New York Pop artist who had reached new levels of international prestige.

NUDES IN PUBLIC

The *Interiors* series inspired the next large commissioned mural that Lichtenstein created for a New York corporate headquarters: *Large Interior with Three Reflections*, a 30-foot-long triptych (with three additional panels) installed at the former Revlon Corporation Building (625 Madison Avenue, between 58th Street and 59th Street). Interestingly, despite his fascination with depicting female emotion in his 1960s comic strip paintings, Lichtenstein had not depicted a female nude in a painting until this one.

Lichtenstein must have grown intrigued with portraying the female nude in his distinctive stylistic idiom. His next series, shown at Castelli's in 1994, depicted female nudes, and in fall 1993 he completed another large sculpture, *Brushstroke Nude*, a 12-foot-high aluminum work that graced the sidewalk in front of the Guggenheim Museum from October 8 through January 16, 1994, welcoming visitors to the Lichtenstein retrospective being held inside. Curated by the artist's longtime friend Diane Waldman, the comprehensive exhibit showcased paintings and sculpture; and it traveled to the Museum of Contemporary Art in Los Angeles before making stops in Montreal, Munich, Hamburg, and Brussels, concluding in Ohio at the Wexner Center for the Arts.

POP ART GOES UNDERGROUND

As a native New Yorker, Roy Lichtenstein was familiar with the city's mass transit system, particularly its infamous subway trains. In 1994, he put forth a visually stunning tribute to one of the city's most enduring institutions with his Times Square Mural, today adorning the mezzanine of the Times Square subway station at 42nd Street.

The idea of commissioning public art for New York's underground transit hubs was formulated as early as 1985, with the establishment by the Mass Transit Authority (MTA) of the Arts for Transit office, charged with providing decorative art elements for the planned refurbishing of many subway and commuter rail stations throughout the 1980s and 1990s. Lichtenstein was offered the commission in 1989, the same year he was given the Mayor's Award of Honor for Art and Culture by Mayor Koch at Gracie Mansion. "I've always thought New York was the center of the universe," the artist told the assembled crowd at Gracie Mansion in his acceptance speech, "so this award has cosmic significance for me." Cosmic significance was also the apparent goal of the work he began sketching the following year.

The black-and-white maquette that formed the core composition of the mural was under way in 1990, but the final version would be delayed for some time, partly due to the city pushing back its renovation of the Times Square station (originally slated for 1992) by two years. At one point, Lichtenstein decided he couldn't wait any longer. As Dorothy recalled years later: "The delay was just so long . . . he just hated the idea of this thing was hanging on, and wasn't completed, in his mind. He said, 'Let's just do it. Then I don't have to think about it anymore.'" Lichtenstein went ahead and transferred the images he had finalized in the maquette to enamel, to exactly the specifications agreed upon for mounting in the underground station.

A child of 1930s New York, Lichtenstein was determined that his subway tribute should echo the themes of that era while looking toward the future. He consulted two books for inspiration. One was *Silver Connections*, a compendium on the history of New York's subways that included detailed drawings of the original ornamentation of the 42nd Street station from 1904. The other was *Buck Rogers: The First 60 Years in the 25th Century*, which familiarized the artist with the Depression-era space hero and his now quaintly outdated fictional future world.

The first section of the mural depicts an arch of old-fashioned tile and masonry, as in the splendid archways of Grand Central Station; the next shows a steel girder representing transportation's evolution in the Machine Age. Standing in for the subway car in the composition is a retro-style rocket ship like one would see in a comic strip or on the cover of a 1920s or 1930s pulp novel. There is even a visual nod to the 1939–40 World's Fair, with a white Trylon poised on the prow of the subway / spaceship slicing through a red Perisphere (two iconic symbols of that fair's "World of Tomorrow" theme). The plaque with the number "42" was recreated from the station's original 1904 decor. *New York Times* writer Avis Berman described the effect of the mural when it was finally unveiled to the public in its intended destination in 2002, nearly five years after Lichtenstein's death:

> The Metropolitan Transportation Authority . . . may rightly see the work as an emblem of a revitalized, forward-looking Times Square. But it's also a Lichtenstein sendup of modernist visions of the future. . . . That [Buck] Rogers appears in the mural, at the far right, as if straight out of a comic book from 1929—when he was

first introduced, six years after Lichtenstein was born in Manhattan—is telling. It underscores that the piece is not so much futuristic as it is retrospective and even nostalgic, evoking a between-the-wars Gotham, when the subways seemed undefiled and the city was being wrenched by industrial and architectural transitions. . . . Read from left to right, "Times Square Subway Mural" portrays a dynamic history of New York urbanism.

As if to emphasize the personal nature of the Times Square project, Lichtenstein, though offered a budget of $200,000, declined to accept any payment from the MTA for his work, saying he "would gladly make it a donation to the city of New York."

"Roy loved New York and rode the subway from the time he was a boy," Dorothy Lichtenstein confirmed at the unveiling in 2002. "He would be so pleased that the mural he created for the Times Square subway station is being installed for the enjoyment of New Yorkers and visitors to his native city." She added, "Roy talked about how unlike the prediction of the future the future really was."

a Shower of accolades

Roy Lichtenstein's predictions for his own future, especially before finding his voice in Pop Art, were likely modest compared with the heights he had attained by his twilight years. The honors and accolades kept coming for him in the mid-1990s. On January 13, 1994, he was honored at the 95th Annual Artists Award Dinner at Manhattan's National Arts Club. Founded in 1898 by Charles de Kay, a longtime art and literary critic for the *New York Times*, the club was conceived as a gathering place for artists and their patrons at the turn of the century—a time when the American art scene was just beginning to turn away from European influences and finding its own energy and inspiration at home. The National Arts Club has been a progressive organization since its inception, always admitting women on an equal basis, and continuing to foster young and minority artists. Its prestigious members include three presidents (Theodore Roosevelt, Woodrow Wilson, and Dwight Eisenhower) and a distinguished roster of artists from all fields, including painters Fredric Remington and William Merritt Chase, sculptor Daniel Chester French, photographer Alfred Stieglitz, and entertainment industry giants Martin Scorcese, Robert Redford, and Dennis Hopper.

Late 1995 brought two major milestones. On October 5, the Lichtensteins traveled to Washington, DC, for a gala ceremony during which Roy was awarded the prestigious National Medal of Arts. And on November 10, the Inamori Foundation of Kyoto, Japan, awarded Lichtenstein its coveted Kyoto Prize.

THE PASSING OF AN ART WORLD GIANT

If his status as a living legend affected Lichtenstein's famous humility and dedication to work, his output in the last few years of his life did not attest to it. As late as 1996, he was exploring new territory. He began a series he called *Landscapes in the Chinese Style*, inspired by an exhibit of the landscapes of Edgar Degas that he had seen at the Met. He also began a series of sculptures based on brushstrokes and drips, and continued to work with the theme of interiors in his so-called Virtual Paintings, where he experimented with colored outlines instead of black. He even returned one more time to two of the muses from his youth, Picasso and Mickey Mouse, in a painting of the Disney character rendered in the artist's Cubist style. The title of the work is *Mickasso*.

Roy Lichtenstein's final exhibition at Leo Castelli's gallery—of his *Landscapes in the Chinese Style*—ran from September 21 to October 26, 1996. His last major outdoor sculpture, *Singapore Brushstrokes*, was installed at Singapore's Pontiac Marina in May 1997. He gave what was his final interview to David Sylvester on April 30 of that year in New York; it was published in the catalog for an exhibition of the artist's *Interiors* paintings at Galerie Lawrence Rubin in Zurich in September. There would be no new Lichtenstein works after that. At the age of seventy-three, the artist contracted pneumonia, and on September 29, 1997, he died of complications from his illness at the New York University Medical Center (550 First Avenue at 31st Street).

Art critics and social commentators across the world contributed obituaries and retrospectives on Lichtenstein's remarkable life and career. Carol Strickland, in the *Christian Science Monitor*, wrote: "For 35 years, he reproduced 20th-century visual icons in a style as machine-like as possible. In so doing, he showed what it means to be human. . . . If Shakespeare's plays 'hold the mirror up to nature,' Roy Lichtenstein makes us look in the mirror of human nature." The *Washington Post*'s Paul Richard commented on the artist's well-known sense of humor, in life and art: "Humor is always problematic in art," he said. "It's like humor in church. Art is very much at ease with suffering and the beauty of the God-created world, but jokes were not considered really permissible. And Lichtenstein was somebody who always had . . . cheery humor in his heart." Jonathan Jones in the *Guardian* summed up Lichtenstein's body of work in the context of his fellow Pop Art icon: "If Warhol made his life a factory, his rival comes across . . . as a pop monk, laboring eternally in a scriptorium of comics."

THE POP GOES ON

New York City remains a living, breathing showcase of Roy Lichtenstein's life and the bold art to which he devoted it. His paintings and sculptures can be found in every major museum in the city, and today's multitude of independent art galleries are the direct result of the role he and his contemporaries played in bringing fine art to the American masses in the 1960s. His public murals and sculptures are an integral part of the city's bustling commercial centers and tourist havens. Michael Bloomberg, another New York mayor with an interest in promoting the arts, joined the Public Arts Fund in sponsoring several public displays of Lichtenstein's sculptures in downtown Manhattan, including *Roy Lichtenstein at City Hall*, a large exhibition in 2003–04. Sculptures such as *Brushstroke Group* (1986) and *Endless Drip* (1995) were displayed in City Hall Park, and the 50-foot-tall *Element E* (1984) was installed in the rotunda of the Department of Education headquarters in the historic Tweed Courthouse.

Today, Dorothy Lichtenstein is the president of the Roy Lichtenstein Foundation, an organization devoted to encouraging greater understanding and appreciation of her husband's work and the art of his time and sharing his artistic legacy with new generations. Headquartered in his last Greenwich Village studio on Washington Street, the foundation was established in 1999, and today works to facilitate the lending of artwork to various institutions. It has taken part in dozens of gallery exhibitions, museum shows, and long-term art loans, and has contributed information to numerous catalogs, symposia, and scholarly articles.

Sadly, as noted at the outset of this book, the foundation has also acquired a reputation in certain circles for being uncooperative, even obstructive, to some scholars and enthusiasts, and its lawyers have forced a number of authors to abandon their projects. As a consequence, the man and his work are less well understood than might otherwise be the case. Happily, however, Lichtenstein's work speaks for itself and can be found across the Internet and in numerous museums, many of them in New York.

Dorothy once recalled something her husband had remarked to her about the afterlife: "He used to joke that he was going to leave his soul to science." One thing is certain: he left a large part of it behind in the city he loved.

NOTES

CHAPTER 1

Page 3: "Roy was always trying to get back . . .": Martin Gayford, "Whaam! Suddenly Roy Was the Darling of the Art World," *Telegraph*, February 23, 2004.

CHAPTER 2

Page 13: "I like making dissonances . . .": Susan Morgan, "A Few Good Colors Are Plenty: Has It Really Been 30 Years Since Roy Lichtenstein First Brought Us Those Cartoon Paintings? Well, Yes. And Now Take a Guided Tour with the Artist Through His Life, Times and All Those Dots," *Los Angeles Times*, January 30, 1994.

Page 18: "You'd get a very strong afterimage . . .": quoted by I. Dervaux, "Baked Potatoes, Hot Dogs, and Girls' Romances: Roy Lichtenstein's Master Drawings," in I. Dervaux (ed.), *Roy Lichtenstein: The Black and White Drawings, 1961–1968* (New York: Morgan Library & Museum, 2010).

Page 22: "After spotting Lichtenstein's talent . . .": Alastair Sooke, "Is Lichtenstein a great modern artist or a copy cat?" BBC.com, Culture, October 21, 2014.

CHAPTER 3

Page 32: "As Kennedy understood . . .": Lisa Phillips, *The American Century*, *1950–2000* (New York: Whitney Museum of American Art, 1999).

Page 34: "Roy Lichtenstein . . . recognizes the faces . . .": Larry Campbell, "Roy Lichtenstein," *ARTNews*, May 1951.

Page 37: "truly like the doodling of a five-year-old": "Is It Art, or Dizzy? Town's in a Tizzy," *Cleveland News*, March 13, 1952.

Page 38: "the most vigorous and original movement in art in the history of the nation": Harold Rosenberg, "The American Action Painters," *ARTNews*, December 1952.

Page 39: ""If twenty years ago paintings . . .": Fairfield Porter, "Lichtenstein's Adult Primer," *ARTNews*, March 1954.

Page 39: "I was taking the stodgy pictures . . ." Quoted in Grace Glueck, "A Pop Artist's Fascination with the First Americans," *New York Times*, December 23, 2005.

Page 51: "Advertising has caused a revolution . . .": Alison and Peter Smithson, "But Today We Collect Ads," *Ark Magazine*, November 1958.

CHAPTER 4

Page 56: "ceased to become paintings and became environments": Allan Kaprow, "The Legacy of Jackson Pollock," *ARTNews*, October 1958.

Page 64: "What is being proposed?": Pierre Restany, "The Nouveau Réalistes Declaration of Intention," *Le Nouveau Réalisme* catalog, October 1960.

Page 65: "That son-of-a-bitch Castelli . . .": Emma Brocks, "Master of Few Words," *Guardian*, July 26, 2004.

Page 67: "The painting presents a scene . . .": Michael Lobel, *Image Duplicator: Roy Lichtenstein and the Emergence of Pop Art* (New Haven: Yale University Press, 2002).

Page 70: "Allan Kaprow . . . called me on the phone . . .": Ivan Karp, interview, Smithsonian Institution Archives of American Art, 1969.

Page 71: "I didn't know who Warhol was . . .": Ivan Karp, interview, 1969.

CHAPTER 5

Page 79: "His comic strip images . . .": David Hopkins, *After Modern Art: 1945–2000* (New York: Oxford University Press, 2000).

Page 80: "None of the beauty that appears . . .": Elizabeth Richardson, "Those Lichtenstein Women," *Harper's Bazaar*, October 1993.

Page 82: "With six decades of work under his belt . . .": Chris Sims, "Russ Heath's comic about being ripped off by Roy Lichtenstein will give you a new appreciation for the Hero Initiative," ComicsAlliance.com, November 7, 2014.

Page 82: "with Oldenburg, Lichtenstein . . .": Max
Kozloff, "Pop Culture, Metaphysical Disgust, and the New
Vulgarians," *Art International*, March 1962.

Page 85: "If people use the word . . .": Dorothy Seiberling,
"Is He the Worst Artist in the US?" *Life*, January 31, 1964.

Page 85: "Well, I was in the middle of a divorce . . .":
Quoted in Richardson, "Those Lichtenstein Women."

Page 90: "By putting a frame around . . .": Les Daniels,
DC Comics: 60 Years of the World's Favorite Comic Book Heroes
(Boston: Little, Brown, 1995).

Page 92: "If you look at the comics . . ." Paul Richard,
"Art's Comic Genius," *Washington Post*, September 30,
1997.

Page 92: "Almost every painting . . .": Rian Hughes, interviewed by Rachael Steven, "Image Duplicator: Pop Art's
Comic Debt," *Creative Review*, May 13, 2013.

Page 93: "The first argument that fills the vacuum . . .":
Brian O'Doherty, "Lichtenstein: Doubtful but Definite
Triumph of the Banal," *New York Times*, October 27, 1963.

CHAPTER 6

Page 99: "As the new landscape . . .": John Canaday, "Pop
Art Sells On and On—Why?" *New York Times Magazine*,
May 31, 1964.

Page 100: "I'm in favor of these things . . .": Seiberling, "Is He the Worst Artist in the US?"

Page 104–105: "The closer my work is to the original . . .": Seiberling, "Is He the Worst Artist in the US?"

Page 108: "They were usually clichés . . .": Richardson, "Those Lichtenstein Women."

Page 108: "Lichtenstein, as dictated by . . .": Unattributed, "Do You Hate Roy Lichtenstein? Then You'll Really Hate This," HeavyMetal.com, 2015.

Page 118: "No, I don't see any signs . . .": Grace Glueck, "Warhol's Pad Is Scene of Blast Launching 'Pop Art,' New Book," *New York Times*, June 30, 1965.

Page 122: "Entering into the spirit . . .": Frank Lloyd Wright, *Architectural Forum*, 1948.

Page 124: "It begins with those earliest paintings . . .": John Canaday, "Art: The Lichtenstein Retrospective," *New York Times*, September 20, 1969.

Page 124: "His first exhibitions . . .": John Canaday, "Roy Lichtenstein and His Great Big Yacht," *New York Times*, September 21, 1969.

Page 125: "I had a thing about clichés . . .": Grace Glueck, "BLAM!! To the Top of the Pop," *New York Times*, September 21, 1969.

CHapter 7

Page 134: "his loveliest and most prepossessing in years . . .": Peter Schjeldahl, "The Artist for Whom 'Style' Is All," *New York Times*, March 21, 1971.

Page 135: "In a sense . . .": Alexi Worth, "From Pop to Now," *ArtForum*, Summer 2002.

Page 144: "Mr. Lichtenstein quite dominates . . .": Hilton Kramer, "Art: 'About Art,' Parodies, at Whitney," *New York Times*, July 21, 1978.

Page 146: "Roy's work was a wonderment formulae . . .": Jack Cowart, interviewed by Alex Beam, "Lichtenstein: Creator or Copycat?" *Boston Globe*, October 18, 2006.

Page 146: "It is important to recognize . . .": Interview with David Barsalou, July 14, 2016.

Page 150: "Moving paint around . . .": Jeff Koons, interview with Martin Gayford, "Artists on Art," *Telegraph*, December 8, 2001.

CHapter 8

Page 156: "The spectator traverses each rectangle . . .": Bernice Rose, *The Drawings of Roy Lichtenstein* (New York: Museum of Modern Art, 1987).

Page 156–157: "There was all this conceptual art around . . .": Dorothy Lichtenstein, quoted in Avis Berman, "In a New Times Square, a Wink at Futures Past," *New York Times*, September 2, 2002.

Page 157: "For the pleasure of the dance": Roy Lichtenstein, quoted in Morgan, "A Few Good Colors Are Plenty."

Page 161: "Benton has a definite social point of view": Quoted in James Rondeau and Sheila Wagstaff, "Introduction, *Roy Lichtenstein: A Retrospective,* exhibition catalog (Chicago: Art Institute of Chicago, 2012).

Page 162: "an indelible sight . . .": Calvin Tomkins, *Roy Lichtenstein: Mural with Blue Brushstroke* (New York: Harry N. Abrams, 1988).

Page 164: "an event of major artistic importance . . .": Michael Brenson, "Art View; Museum and Corporation—A Delicate Balance," *New York Times*, February 23, 1986.

Page 164: "It's supposed to be humorous . . .": Roy Lichtenstein, quoted in "The Art Behind the Dots," *New York Times Magazine*, March 8, 1987.

Page 169: "Mr. Lichtenstein's Nike of Samothrace . . .": Michael Brenson, "Cityful of Sculpture under the Sky," *New York Times*, July 26, 1991.

Page 171: "I've always thought New York . . .": Berman, "In a New Times Square, a Wink at Futures Past."

Page 171: "The delay was just so long . . .": Dorothy Lichtenstein, quoted in Berman, "In a New Times Square, a Wink at Futures Past."

Page 172–173: "The Metropolitan Transportation Authority . . ." Berman, "In a New Times Square, a Wink at Futures Past."

Page 173: "Roy loved New York . . .": Dorothy Lichtenstein, quoted in Berman, "In a New Times Square, a Wink at Futures Past."

Page 175: "For 35 years . . .": Carol Strickland, "Roy Lichtenstein: Keen Observer of Life's Little Ironies," *Christian Science Monitor*, October 3, 1997.

Page 176: "Humor is always problematic . . .": Paul Richard, "Art's Comic Genius," *Washington Post*, September 30, 1997.

Page 176: "If Warhol made his life a factory . . .": Jonathan Jones, "Comic Stripped," *Guardian*, January 6, 2004.

Page 177: "He used to joke . . .": Dorothy Lichtenstein in an interview with Agnes Gund, Museum of Modern Art Oral History Project, May 6, 1998.

CAPTIONS AND CREDITS

Pages ii–iii: New York City in the 1960s. © iStock / Lisa-Blue.

Facing page 1: Times Square in 1973. Photograph by Dan McCoy for the Environmental Protection Agency. U.S. National Archives and Records Administration, record 2389842, via Wikimedia Commons.

Page 8: The opening panels from the very first comic strip featuring Buck Rogers, one of the young Lichtenstein's favorite comic heroes. From Philip Nowlan (script) and Richard Calkins (illustration), "Armageddon 2419 A.D," in *Amazing Stories,* January 7, 1929.

Page 30: The tide of postwar consumerism was accompanied by a surge in advertising. This early 1960s ad for Arm and Hammer may be the inspiration for Lichtenstein's *The Refrigerator.* David Barsalou kindly provided this image.

Page 46: An illustration by comics artist Tony Abruzzo that may be the inspiration for Lichtenstein's *Portrait of Ivan Karp* (the director of the Leo Castelli Gallery) and *Portrait of Allan Kaprow* (the avante-garde pioneet of Happenings). The two portraits were done in Lichtenstein's emerging cartoon style, and neither subject looks much like Karp or Kaprow. David Barsalou kindly provided this image.

Page 73: This advertisement for the Mount Airy Lodge ran in many New York–area newspapers in the early 1960s. It may be the source for Lichtenstein's *Girl with Ball.* David Barsalou kindly provided this image.

Page 74: This square-jawed illustration from a Sunday comic page (summer 1961) by the comics artist Milt Caniff may be the source material for Lichtenstein's *Mr. Bellamy.* David Barsalou kindly provided this image.

Page 96: The 1964 New York World's Fair (advertised here on a postcard from the time) featured murals by ten Pop artists, including Lichtenstein. David Barsalou kindly provided this image.

Page 126: In the 1970s, parts of New York became squalid havens of crime and urban decay. Graffiti was everywhere, not least in the subway, where commuters tried their best to ignore it—as shown in this photo from 1977 of passengers on the Lexington Avenue line. The photograph is by Jim Pickerell, U.S. National Archives and Records Administration, record 4588217, via Wikimedia Commons.

Page 152: The World Trade Center in the 1980s. © iStock / grabi.

INDEX

ABOUT THE AUTHOR

Mark P. Bernardo is a journalist and editor who has written about travel, entertainment, art, culture, and lifestyles for such publications as *Maxim*, *Bloomberg Pursuits*, *Bloomberg Markets*, *Robb Report*, and *Worth*. He was the editor of *Smoke* for six years and is the digital media editor of *WatchTime*. An aficionado of art history and a fixture on the New York City museum scene, Mark's interest in Roy Lichtenstein's work was inspired by the author's previous career as an editor, writer, and color artist for Marvel Comics. Mark's previous books include *Mad Men's Manhattan: The Insider's Guide* and *Elvis Presley: Memphis*. Mark and his wife live in New York's Hudson River Valley.